GROWING A RACE

Growing a Race

Nellie L. McClung and the Fiction of Eugenic Feminism

CECILY DEVEREUX

McGill-Queen's University Press

Montreal & Kingston · London · Ithaca

© McGill-Queen's University Press 2005
ISBN 0-7735-2937-3

Legal deposit fourth quarter 2005
Bibliothèque nationale du Québec

Printed in Canada on acid-free paper that is 100% ancient forest free
(100% post-consumer recycled), processed chlorine free.

This book has been published with the help of a grant from the Canadian
Federation for the Humanities and Social Sciences, through the Aid to
Scholarly Publications Programme, using funds provided by the Social
Sciences and Humanities Research Council of Canada.

McGill-Queen's University Press acknowledges the support of the Canada
Council for the Arts for our publishing program. We also acknowledge
the financial support of the Government of Canada through the Book
Publishing Industry Development Program (BPIDP) for our publishing
activities.

Library and Archives Canada Cataloguing in Publication

Devereux, Cecily Margaret, 1963–
    Growing a race: Nellie L. McClung and the fiction
of eugenic feminism/Cecily Devereux.

    Includes bibliographical references and index.
    ISBN 0-7735-2937-3

    1. McClung, Nellie, 1873–1951. 2. Eugenics in literature. 3. Feminism
in literature. I. Title.

PS8525.C52Z6 2005   813'.52   C2005-906016-6

Typeset in Sabon 10.5/13
by Infoscan Collette, Quebec City

For my mother, Joan Devereux

Contents

Acknowledgments

The debts I have incurred in producing this study are numerous. Staff at the Provincial Archives of British Columbia helped me to locate materials in McClung's voluminous holdings and elsewhere in the archives. John Charles and Jeannine Green at the Bruce Peel Special Collections at the University of Alberta were endlessly generous with their time and assistance. I would also like to thank the librarians and staff at the D.B. Weldon Library at the University of Western Ontario, the United Church Archives in Toronto, and the Metro Reference Library. Many colleagues and friends have been involved in this study in various ways, and I am grateful for the comments and suggestions offered by Misao Dean, Janice Fiamengo, Carole Gerson, Chris Gittings, Tracy Kulba, Susan Hamilton, Paul Hjartarson, Ian MacLaren, Barbara MacLean, Jean LeDrew-Metcalfe, Peter and Hilary Neary, Paul Potts, Julie Rak, Mark Simpson, Stephen Slemon, and Jo-Ann Wallace. Thomas Tausky, who died in 2001, bore with my agonizing over the project in its early days, and his balanced judgment and clear thinking have ultimately tempered much of my discussion of McClung's writing. My family endured the numerous side-effects of my research and writing: as always, extra special thanks to Scott, Lucy, and Susan Wright, and to Joan, Joanna, Jeremy, and Benet Devereux. Finally, I wish to gratefully acknowledge the support of the Social Sciences and Humanities Research Council of Canada and of the Faculty of Arts, Support for the Advancement of Scholarship, at the University of Alberta.

GROWING A RACE

I cannot look back without regret. I can see too many places where I could have been more obedient to the heavenly vision, for a vision I surely had for the creation of a better world.

Nellie McClung, *The Stream Runs Fast*

McClung in the Third Wave
Revisiting the "Legacy"

In any society, the citizens who bring about improvement in the human condition are those crusaders who are committed to change. Canada has produced a broad, and colorful, spectrum of dedicated Activists – from Prairie populists to Quebec separatists – and, as *Maclean's* sees it, the most important was a tireless advocate who led the campaign for women's rights.

> "100 Most Important Canadians in History:
> Activists: Nellie McClung," *Maclean's*, 1 July 1998

Eugenics found most of its champions in the western provinces. In 1928 Alberta passed its own sexual sterilization act aimed at the so-called feeble-minded. British Columbia followed suit in 1933, the same year the Nazis came to power in Germany. Some of the most vocal advocates were progressive women such as Nellie McClung.

> Lynn Glazier, CBC *Sunday Morning*, September 1992

Nellie L. McClung (1873–1951) is English Canada's best-known feminist of the period that is usually, if inaccurately in the context of the long and global history of the struggle for gender equality, referred to as the "First Wave." The most influential figure in the achievement of provincial woman suffrage in Manitoba in 1916, McClung was also instrumental in the passage in 1917 of legislation providing limited federal enfranchisement for women who were relatives of members of the armed forces, and, subsequently, in 1918, for all women. (The Dominion Elections Act was passed in 1920, reaffirming and making permanent woman suffrage in Canada, as well as providing women with eligibility to hold office. See Cleverdon, 2.¹) McClung played a central role in the constitutional and national legislation of gender and citizenship as one of the "Famous Five" in the 1929 "Persons Case," which led to the reinterpretation of the British North America (BNA) Act to include women as "persons."[2] Although the most obvious effect of the "Persons Case" was the entry of women into the Canadian Senate, it had much broader implications in giving women the "rights and privileges" of personhood, as well as what they had always had in British North America and Canada, the "duties and responsibilities."

These reforms are the best-known aspects of what McClung herself has represented as her "legacy" (1945, xiii).[3] But her accomplishments were many and remarkable. Veronica Strong-Boag, in her introduction to the 1972 University of Toronto Press reprint of McClung's 1915 suffrage manifesto, *In Times Like These*, points out that, in addition to her suffrage and BNA Act work, McClung was "the only woman at the Canadian War Conference of 1918, an MLA in Alberta [from 1921 to 1926], and the first woman to represent Canadian Methodism at a World Ecumenical Conference [in 1921]. In 1936 she became the first woman member of the Canadian Broadcasting Corporation's Board of Governors and in 1938 a Canadian delegate to the League of Nations [precursor of the United Nations]. Sixteen books and numerous articles made her one of Canada's best-known authors. Working with press clubs and the Canadian Authors Association, she was a strong exponent of cultural nationalism" (vii).

Moreover, as an elected Liberal member for the Alberta provincial legislative assembly between 1921 and 1926, McClung fought for and succeeded in helping to bring about changes to the divorce act, the dower act, and the married women's property act in Alberta. A speech by McClung, dated 31 January 1924, shows her taking a strong position on these matters in the legislature, arguing that "the disabilities [married women] labor under in regard to their property [is] the last relic of barbarism which sullies our laws" (PABC 25.7 4). She pushed successfully for the entry of women into what were non-traditional fields: she "spearheaded," as Marilyn I. Davis observes, "the fight for the ordination of theologically qualified women in the United Church of Canada" (1996, 14), and helped to open up Canadian politics to female representatives. Indeed, she was a powerful advocate for working women and the expansion of women's careers generally, as well as for their fair remuneration at a time when women in Canada were paid considerably less than men for any work at all, and when marriage and children could be grounds for their dismissal from employment.[4] She occupied a prominent public position as a politician and as a writer. During the suffrage years she was a speaker in great demand in the United States as well as in Canada. Records among her papers at the Provincial Archives of British Columbia show her to have kept up a gruelling whistle-stop campaign in the United States and to have had more invitations to speak there than she could accept.

In addition to the suffrage cause and women's rights, McClung spoke and wrote about temperance, birth control, immigration, domestic "missionary" work, and international relations. For many of the issues she took up, through her newspaper and magazine writing, she functioned as a recognizable and popular spokesperson. She corresponded with numerous people, including prime ministers Robert Borden and Mackenzie King, "Famous Five" member Emily Murphy, writers Irene Baird, James Oliver Curwood, William Arthur Deacon, and Laura Goodman Salverson, as well as dozens of lesser-known friends. In addition to her suffrage book, *In Times Like These* (1915), McClung published four novels, *Sowing Seeds in Danny* (1908), *The Second Chance* (1910), *Purple Springs* (1921), and *Painted Fires* (1925); two novellas, *The Black Creek Stopping-House and Other Stories* (1912) and *When Christmas Crossed "The Peace"* (1923); a co-written story of a Canadian soldier's escape from a German prison camp, *Three Times and Out* (1918); and four books of short stories and short pieces, *The Next of Kin* (1917), *All We Like Sheep* (1930), *Be Good to Yourself* (1930), and *Flowers for the Living* (1931). She also published two collections of articles from her syndicated newspaper column, *Leaves from Lantern Lane* (1936) and *More Leaves from Lantern Lane* (1937), as well as two volumes of autobiography, *Clearing in the West* (1935) and *The Stream Runs Fast* (1945). By any measure, her achievements were impressive. Considering that when she began her career women in Canada were disenfranchised, not constitutionally "persons," and strictly limited in a range of statutory and legislated ways from earning a livelihood, owning property, and keeping custody of their children or assets in divorce proceedings or inheritance, her work should appear to be extraordinary.

At the beginning of the twenty-first century, however, Nellie McClung is a figure whose feminist "legacy" to English Canada is characterized, as Janice Fiamengo has observed, by ambivalence.[5]

On the one hand, McClung is regularly valorized in popular historical representations as a national hero who, in the shape of what
Norman P. Lambert in 1916 called "a Joan of the West," led Canadian women to provincial and federal enfranchisement and personhood and the nation to "a new and enlarged democracy" (265).
The CRB Foundation's "Heritage Minute" is one example of these
representations;[6] her figuring prominently on millennial "Top Ten
Canadians" lists is another.[7] On the other hand, McClung is now
just as regularly castigated as she is praised for her part in Canadian
history. Like her friend Emily Murphy, she has come to be increasingly known as a supporter of the 1928 Sexual Sterilization Bill in
Alberta, which, until 1972, empowered a board of four members
to inhibit, through surgical sterilization, "the power of procreation"
for anyone residing in a provincial institution deemed a "mentally
defective person" (*Revised Statutes of Alberta* 1942, 2448). Media
reports on the bill and its history arising from Leilani Muir's successful 1995 action against the Alberta government for her sterilization in 1958 at the age of fourteen drew widespread popular
attention for the first time to the involvement of McClung and
Murphy as early and influential supporters of eugenical legislation.[8]
Many accounts of the Muir action and its historical circumstances
specifically noted these two women;[9] some imputed to them a primary agency in the passage of the bill. One report, for example,
claimed that, "In Alberta, the leaders of the [eugenics] movement
were suffragette Nellie McClung and legendary feminist Emily
Murphy, first woman magistrate in the British Empire" (*Western
Report* 10, no. 24 [1995]).[10]

   "Eugenics" was the name given in 1883 by British scientist Francis
Galton for what he was developing as a "science" of selective breeding or "judicious mating." The basis of eugenics was genetic, the idea
that many characteristics or "tendencies" – not only physical characteristics but perceived inclinations towards, for instance, alcoholism, tuberculosis, or insanity – are hereditary. The logic of selective
breeding suggested that if "bad" characteristics could be blocked and
"good" ones fostered, the quality of a nation's people, or its "race,"
could be improved, made individually and collectively stronger and
healthier, and thus the nation itself would be made more powerful.
Galton's ideas of eugenics are most readily comprehensible in relation to the kind of ethnic nationalism that Eric Hobsbawm has
traced in the years between 1880 and 1914. After 1880, Hobsbawm

has suggested, in most national contexts, "ethnicity and language became the central, increasingly the decisive or even the only criteria of potential nationhood" (1990, 102). Underpinning Galtonian eugenics was an impulse to refine and strengthen a nation conceived in these terms, as an identifiable *racial* community whose preservation was necessary to the protection of a particular geopolitical space. In the British Empire these terms also pertained to colonial space as an extension of the central imperial nation (the "Greater Britain"). Imperialism after 1880 was based on the same criterion of preserving a category understood as "race" and on the same notion of strengthening nation. Indeed, empire-building makes national strength all the more urgently required for maintaining the home "stock" while also populating colonized territory with nationally identifiable settlers.

Angus McLaren has suggested in his 1990 study, *Our Own Master Race: Eugenics in Canada, 1885–1945*, that the study of "judicious mating" was less a science of breeding than a biological politics that undertook to improve the quality of one ethnic category by encouraging limited and selective reproduction and by eliminating what was seen to be "defective" from the breeding stock (127).[11] The Alberta bill was praised at the time of its discussion and passage as, according to the *Eugenical News* in 1928, "purely eugenical" (47). In recent years it has been widely condemned as a racist initiative, which located "defectiveness," as McLaren indicates, in racial categories. McLaren cites statistics presented by Timothy J. Christian demonstrating that under the bill "a disproportionate number of Roman Catholic and Greek Orthodox patients were treated. Among those both approved for and ultimately sterilized, eastern Europeans were overrepresented and Anglo-Saxons underrepresented. But the clearest evidence that differential treatment was meted out by the Alberta Board of Eugenics is provided by an examination of its care of Indian and Métis patients. In the last years of the Board's activities, Indian and Métis, who represented only 2.5 per cent of Alberta's population, accounted for over 25 per cent of those sterilized" (160). Similarly disturbing numbers pertaining to the national origins of patients admitted to the Provincial Mental Hospital in Ponoka, Alberta, in 1928 are presented by Terry Chapman in a 1977 article in *Alberta History*. Chapman argues that Alberta's legislation of eugenical sterilization represents one response to "the massive immigration experienced by western Canada prior to

1914" and must thus always be understood, with assimilation, as a "means to ensure that Canada would forever remain white, Anglo-Saxon and Protestant" (10).[12]

Since the media reports of their support for eugenics legislation, it has become commonplace to observe that McClung and Murphy were racists, a description that does not characterize their representation in the early twentieth century or at the time of the discussions pertaining to the Sexual Sterilization Bill in Alberta.[13] During ceremonies commemorating the Famous Five and the Persons Case in Calgary in 1999, a number of media reports drew renewed attention to the politics of race that had been foregrounded in the Muir action and that Governor-General Adrienne Clarkson had negotiated in her speech at the ceremony's unveiling of new statues of the Five. *Calgary Herald* columnist Naomi Lakritz, for instance, wrote in response to Clarkson's suggestion that the Famous Five were "women of their time" and that the new monument "stands for diversity and equality": "Um – sorry, Your Worship, but it stands for nothing of the kind. The didactic beliefs about white superiority, yellow perils and even eugenics that marked this quintet are neither democratic nor nation-building, and have nothing to do with diversity and equality" (19 October 1999).[14] Lakritz notes Emily Murphy's anti-Asian sentiments, to which *Globe and Mail* reporter Jan Wong had drawn attention at a luncheon in Calgary held by the Famous Five Foundation a year earlier. Wong, Joe Woodward reports, had read from Murphy's 1922 book, *The Black Candle*, in which, he suggests, Murphy "accused Canada's Chinese of conniving in 'the downfall of the white race' with their opium" (30).

The *Black Candle* is now frequently cited on these terms, as a racist text that made a case against a traffic in drugs by reminding its readers of the dangers such a traffic imposes upon Anglo-Saxons and Anglo-Saxon dominance. Noting the "tendency" of opium addicts "to become impotent," Murphy wrote, a well-known British eugenist, Dr C.W. Saleeby, "has recently pointed out that in Great Britain in 1919, for the first time, the deaths have actually exceeded the births. He also points out that there are more Germans in Germany than there are Britons in the whole of our Empire, and contends that in a generation or so, these prolific Germans, with the equally prolific Russians, and the still more fertile yellow races, will wrest the leadership of the world from the British" (46–7).[15]

"Wise folk," Murphy grimly concluded, "ought to think about these things for a while" (47). What this passage indicates, of course, is the extent to which Murphy's concerns about trafficking in drugs are motivated by anxiety about the health and the "leadership" of the category of the imperial "race" rather than, for example, individual well-being of members of a national community understood under any other terms. In this *The Black Candle* is like McClung's well-known campaign for prohibition and temperance which, similarly, argued against a traffic in alcohol in part on the basis of its effects as what Saleeby called a "racial poison," a substance seen to act adversely through the individual upon a particular category understood as a race. Indeed, both campaigns are readily comprehensible as eugenic measures: they are undertaken to "conserve the race" by eliminating "poisons" that diminish the strength of the national community.

Murphy's association with the wrongs of eugenics legislation and of what she referred to as "the mental and physical betterment of our racial life" (*Vancouver Sun*, 3 September 1932) has been a major issue in the ongoing commemoration of her work as a fighter for the rights of women. This is the case even though – or perhaps because – that valorization has been accelerated in the past decade with the formation of the Famous Five Foundation in 1996, the circulation of celebratory vignettes on television such as the CRB Foundation's Heritage Minutes, and the heightened popular awareness of the Famous Five through such national undertakings as their appearance in 2001 on the back of the Canadian $50 bill. The outcry over the naming of a transition house for abused women and children in Vancouver is a case in point. In response to objections about calling the house after Murphy, the North Shore Crisis Services Society changed the originally proposed name to SAGE (for Shelter, Advocacy, Growth, and Empowerment) House. This decision was made, according to Laura Reynolds of the society, because "Murphy 'held very definite racist views and was very vocal in her opinions regarding eugenics'" (*British Columbia Report* 9, no. 38 [1998] 30).[16]

"For the same reasons [of racism]," Sabitri Ghosh noted in the *Catholic New Times* in 1999, Canada's main feminist organization, "the National Action Committee on the Status of Women (NAC) decided not to support the placement of a Famous Five monument on Parliament Hill." Ghosh quotes NAC president Joan Grant-Cummings: "Our reaction comes out of the feedback we got from Aboriginal women, women of colour, disabled women ... We find it quite offensive because yes, these so-called 'Famous Five' advanced women's rights, but it was done in a very partial way, in a racist way, in a classist and ablist way" (10). Grant-Cummings notably dissociates herself and the NAC from the Famous Five, and in the process marks a shift in feminist thinking in English Canada. Her comments emphasize the extent to which, in the context of such encounters between feminist history and contemporary Canadian society, first-wave figures such as McClung and Murphy have come to be regarded with growing suspicion, especially by feminists of the so-called third wave or postfeminist period.

Second-wave feminists in the 1960s and '70s embraced predecessors such as McClung and Murphy as "foremothers," seeing in them the signs of a continuum and the roots of a tradition, even while they noted their ideological shortcomings (they did not go far enough politically; they were too invested in motherhood and patriarchy). Later twentieth-century feminists, however, sought to distance themselves from women whose work for equal rights for women is so demonstrably focused on a white constituency and whose politics of gendered empowerment are so clearly based on ideas of race and racial superiority. Many post-imperial, "third-wave" feminist critiques have argued that white women emerged in the late nineteenth and early twentieth centuries as political agents only through the disempowerment of constituencies that are constructed as "others," along axes of race and class in particular.[17] In Canada this disempowerment is apparent in the eugenical measures in which women such as Murphy and McClung were involved, and for which they have come to be known as the leaders.

McClung and Murphy do not differ in any significant way from other first-wave feminists working in imperial contexts. They were certainly what is now defined as racist. As they saw a need to preserve a society that was to be characterized by its "race," social reform for them was also always "racial" reform; social progress in early twentieth-century English Canada was also always the advancement of the Anglo-Saxon empire of Great Britain. They supported the eugenical legislation of the Alberta Sexual Sterilization Bill that led to the surgical sterilization of nearly three thousand people, disproportionate numbers of whom were not Anglo-Saxon.

Moreover, the legislation was based on a notion of national community that did not include a disabled citizenship.[18] Murphy made alarmist statements about Asian migrants in Canada. McClung supported assimilative "home missions" work for non-Anglo-Saxon Canadian immigrants and residential schools for First Nations children.

The advancement of women that McClung and Murphy both sought to effect depended on the construction of categories of people as infantilized, backward, less evolved, needing "uplift," requiring assimilation into "Canadianness." Their conception of "Canadianness" was rooted in British imperial ideas of race and of natural racial hierarchies and in what Antoinette Burton has characterized for first-wave white feminists in India and other imperial contexts as "the white woman's burden" to "raise up" the "lower" races (1992). Thus, from the perspective of late twentieth and early twenty-first century English Canada, McClung and Murphy represent a history of racial prejudice and repressive ideas of a "white Canada." From their own perspective, however, they were progressive; their activism for women and for social reform put them at the forefront of workers for what is still represented as "progress" in the early twentieth century. They were, in effect, in their time, the moral and social equivalent of their own late twentieth-century critics, believing themselves to be working towards liberating women from oppressive conditions and moving all people towards a better nation than the one they had inherited.[19]

That this nation was *not* better and that it has continued to be profoundly and systemically exclusionary and oppressive for many Canadians makes contentious and difficult a reassessment of figures such as McClung and Murphy and the question of where and how they should be located and understood. McClung, like Murphy a supporter of eugenic ideas, a representative of a politics of racialized maternal feminism, an advocate of cultural assimilation, is in the untenable position of being an agent of a particular kind of social and national work for which she cannot be unproblematically commemorated. Like so many feminists of the first wave, she is understood to have paradoxically done "good" work for many women that is "bad" because it took place within a framework of cultural imperialism. Contemporary critical evaluations have tended to negotiate this paradox by swinging between a sense that it is "inappropriate to judge a woman like McClung by contemporary standards"

(Fiamengo 1999–2000, 83) and a sense that a woman like McClung *must* be judged by contemporary standards because she figures at this time as a national hero. Neither approach is entirely satisfactory, the first because it seems to suggest that the ideas of earlier generations cannot be properly assessed or that they *should* not be assessed, the second because it leads to a kind of historical denial and to a serious overwriting and reconfiguration of a problematic past. When figures such as Emily Murphy are *not* named, as in the case of SAGE House, they are to all intents and purposes erased from historical signification, their presence in the past displaced by an imperative to move beyond the effects and residues of that history.

McClung was certainly a figure of her own time. The context within which her feminism must be understood is one that it is possible to analyze and assess morally from the perspective of having seen the results of early twentieth-century policies of assimilation, white protectionism, and eugenical legislation. But it is also important to consider how the ideas held by McClung, as well as by other supporters of eugenics, were believed to have the greatest social good as their objective. The Canada that many social reformers imagined would be a better place would not only be more efficient and productive in economic terms; it would be gentler and safer for everyone. This consideration is not simply a matter of imputing to her and her contemporaries "good intentions" (although such an argument is often made). What is clear in McClung's writing is that, for her, controlling reproduction – the basis of eugenics – was crucial to liberating women, improving social conditions, protecting what seemed to her to be weaker or needier members of society, and maintaining national economic strength in what was imagined, if never actually realized, as a community organized around principles of "common good." Eugenics was not for her and her contemporaries a "bad" measure adopted for a "good" end but a spectrum of "solutions" to perceived problems in the national community. It would ultimately include sexual sterilization in Alberta and British Columbia, but its central premises were birth control, sexual education for men and women, instruction and support for mothers, and the empowerment of women to implement these premises. These were the measures supported by many first-wave feminists, and they do not differ notably from many ideas still circulating in the later twentieth and twenty-first centuries.

One obvious parallel between ideas of the early twentieth century and the early twenty-first can be seen in the continuing debate about abortion rights in North America. McClung's case for controlling reproduction to protect mothers, living children, and society anticipates pro-choice feminist rhetoric, particularly the slogan, "Every child a wanted child; every mother a willing mother": "When the time comes, as it is surely coming, when no child comes into life unwelcomed and unwanted; when systems of State clinics and State hospitals spread their wholesome and healing gospel of good health for all; when mothers have time to enjoy and know their children, and time to study their growing minds; when the Church takes up the great problems of teaching people how to live with as much earnestness as it has tried to show them how to die, the family will be exalted and glorified" ("Keeping Friends with the Family," in *Be Good to Yourself*, 118). McClung's argument here, typical of first-wave reform feminism, resonates with concern less about individual women and freedom of choice – as in later twentieth-century feminist rhetoric – than about the family as the representative unit of the national community and the mother as the centre of that unit and that community. Reproduction was to be controlled for the strengthening of the family and for the betterment of the nation understood as the political and territorial locus of "the race."

McClung, like Murphy, saw the eugenic ideas she endorsed as measures that were fundamentally opposed to the ideas then circulating in, for instance, Germany, while sharing with them a "scientific" basis. "Germany," McClung suggested in *Maclean's* in 1916, "conserves its population for the purpose of destruction, it seems; to establish a world dominion. We should do equally well with ours, but for a far better, nobler motive. We want to grow a race of men and women whose purpose will be life and growth – not death and destruction" (July 1916, 38). McClung's notion of "growing a race" underpins what was in her view a benevolent nationalism within what many Canadians would still regard as a sound imperial project of social reform well after the Second World War. Her support of protected motherhood is the basis for what was in her view a radical feminism that fought for the recognition of women as full citizens. The fact that in recent years many Canadians do not take her point of view should not result inevitably in the overwriting of her work or the downplaying of her part in the construction of the English-Canadian nation in the years around the two world wars, but rather in an effort to understand it.

Ian Dowbiggin makes the point in a 1998 *Globe and Mail* commentary that "until we come to grips with our own present and highly imperfect past, we should be wary about smearing the reputations of Canadians [like McClung] from a bygone era" (3 July 1998). Constance Backhouse issues a similar caution: early feminists "waged battles to advance women's cause, and paid a price for challenging portions of the patriarchal system ... A new generation of feminists may criticize our efforts and find us similarly wanting, in part for errors that we ought to have recognized ourselves, and in part for failure to move in directions that we can only faintly imagine" (1991, 4). McClung and Murphy, as Backhouse and Dowbiggin both suggest, worked within political and ideological constraints that should be taken into account since there are always such constraints in operation – and, indeed, since some of the political and ideological positions of early twentieth-century feminists persist into the present. In both comments it is implicit that what is at stake in critiques of first-wave feminism and its eugenical work is the present and not the past. That is, it is what this work means to contemporary Canada that matters, and how it signifies in relation to the ongoing construction of national community and identity that is a problem that needs to be addressed now. The disjunctions between early twentieth-century social reform feminism and later twentieth-century feminist politics continue to need more scholarly analysis if they are to be understood. The investment of first-wave feminism in eugenics is not easily explained, and it is clearly often difficult for "third-wave" feminists not to take an oppositional position to the earlier politics. Given what some critics see as the rupturing of feminism from its own history that is the western postfeminist condition, and the extent to which feminism cannot at this time coherently address gender-based inequalities on a global scale,[20] and given that McClung and her contemporaries are most often now identified *first* in terms of eugenics and racial politics, it is this connection that needs continued attention.

In 1987, Susan Jackel noted that there was no full-length study of McClung's fiction. In 1993, there was one: Randi R. Warne's *Literature as Pulpit: The Christian Social Activism of Nellie L. McClung*. Warne's book was the first to situate McClung's fiction in relation to her feminism clearly and compellingly as a strand of the social gospel and social reform movements. Like Marilyn I. Davis and Mary Hallett's scholarly biographical treatment, *Firing the Heather: The Life and Times of Nellie McClung* (1994), and the work of second-wave feminists who sought to align themselves with the "pioneering" first wave, *Literature as Pulpit* does not specifically address the engagement of McClung's feminism with eugenical ideas. McClung was English Canada's most influential feminist of the early century, and an important figure in North American suffrage feminism, speaking for the cause of enfranchisement for women throughout the United States as well as Canada. She was one of English Canada's best-known and most popular writers of fiction for at least half of the twentieth century. In the wake of her second-wave recuperation and her continuing representation as a national hero, her writing is slowly reappearing in print.[21] Although several studies of first-wave feminism have drawn attention to the investment of McClung's work in a politics of ethnic nationalism, race-based social reform, and Anglo-imperialism, there has been no sustained study of her fiction that considers it in these terms.[22] It is this gap that the present study attempts to close. It joins existing studies of McClung's politics in locating the crux of her feminism in ideas of maternalism; it differs from existing studies of McClung's feminism in reconsidering the extent to which her maternal feminism can be understood as what British eugenist Caleb Saleeby called "Eugenic Feminism," and her work for eugenical reform to have been undertaken in her fiction. It does not undertake to restore McClung to an unproblematized national heroism, nor to redeem the racist politics of first-wave feminism, but rather to understand McClung's fiction in terms of its engagement with these politics and what they have meant for the nation early twentieth-century feminists sought to build, as well as to the national condition of a post-feminism that they continue to inform and shape.

This study of McClung is concerned with questions of the ways in which contemporary feminism remains attached to earlier feminist discourse and in which contemporary Canadians embrace or reject figures such as McClung, apparently endorsing or opposing her politics of race *or* her politics of gender, but not functionalizing the two together. In this work, I have been motivated by questions about McClung and her oddly ambivalent representation in popular and academic writing, as well as by "third-wave" feminist responses to her. What does it mean to characterize eugenics in Canada as a movement "led" by feminists? And to concomitantly characterize first-wave feminism as a movement that is tainted and undermined by its involvement in the full spectrum of eugenical ideas, from birth control and the protection of mothers to the sterilization of the putatively "unfit"? Why *did* feminists embrace the fundamentally anti-feminist ideas of eugenics? Are women judged, in embracing eugenics, more harshly than male eugenists? If this happens, is it because the notion that women are morally superior and naturally caregivers – the idea that underpins first-wave feminism – continues to circulate in early twentieth-century gender ideologies? Is feminism ever not eugenic? Is race preservation along national and imperial lines a constant in the discourse of gender rights? If so, what does the investment in ideas of race along any axis mean for feminism? Is there a place for McClung in feminist study now – and is it worth defining? What will be gained?

I cannot claim to have answered all these questions in this study, which, after all, considers only one small part of what is understood by feminism and feminist writing of the early twentieth century. But I do feel that these larger issues are the study's real concern, and that the work, if not of establishing an imagined and coherent feminist continuum or of an imagined global feminism, at least of productive engagement with an often objectionable past, *is* important to twenty-first century feminist discourse and practice. I do not want to valorize the past or to reproduce it but to understand it and to continue to work for what is not, despite some postfeminist argument and the persistent rhetoric of "progress," actually evident in Canada – that is, gender equality across all social registers; recognition of the implications of race and class in the social construction of particular categories of womanhood; and a social system that reconciles the representation of motherhood as a sacred duty with real support. It is in relation to these questions that this study undertakes to reread and to reassess McClung's fiction, and to reconsider the narratives and representations of her vision of a feminist "new world" and of a "race" maintained through the public intervention of women into the operation of the state.

PART ONE

"To Serve and Save the Race"
McClung, Maternal Feminism, and the Principles of Eugenics

The woman movement, which has been scoffed and jeered at and misunderstood most of all by the people whom it is destined to help, is a spiritual revival of the best instincts of womanhood – the instinct to serve and save the race.

McClung, *In Times Like These*

I

Changing Perspectives of Maternal Feminism

Reconsidering the "New Woman" and the "Mother of the Race"

Women, this is our day to effectively stay the ravages of war, plague
and famine. This is pre-eminently, and as never before, the day when
the hand that rocks the cradle is called to its mission of ruling
the world.

> Emily Murphy, *Vancouver Sun*, 1 October 1932

Too long have the gentle ladies sat in their boudoirs looking at life in
a mirror like the Lady of Shallot, while down below, in the street, the
fight rages, and other women, and defenceless children, are getting the
worst of it. But the cry is going up to the boudoir ladies to come down
and help us, for the battle goes sorely; and many there are who are
throwing aside the mirror and coming out where the real things are.
The world needs the work and help of the women, and the women
must work, if the race will survive.

> McClung, *In Times Like These*

In 1915, Nellie McClung, already a popular writer of fiction and
familiar figure on the Canadian literary scene, published in book
form the arguments she had become well known for presenting in
speeches for woman suffrage in English Canada. Appearing only a
year before Manitoba became the first province in Canada to enfran-
chise women, *In Times Like These* was influential in circulating
these arguments through the provinces and in achieving the federal
vote in 1920 for Canadian women. It arguably had some effect on
female enfranchisement even outside of Canada: the book was

published in the United States as well as in Canada, and was read in Britain.[1] Still in print at the beginning of the twenty-first century, following its 1972 reissue, *In Times Like These* remains a classic text of first-wave feminism in imperial contexts, like and with other works such as Olive Schreiner's *Woman and Labour* (1911) and Charlotte Perkins Gilman's *The Man-Made World or, Our Andro-centric Culture* (1911). McClung makes numerous references to both in her writing.

In *Times Like These* is also the clearest sustained articulation in English Canada of the politics of what is usually characterized as "maternal feminism." Like Gilman's and Schreiner's texts, it built its case for the female vote on the basis of a conception of women's moral superiority to men that was understood, as many historians of the period have observed, to be a direct and inevitable result of sexual difference and an effect of a biologically explained maternal instinct.[2] "Deeply rooted in every woman's heart," McClung maintained, "is the love and care of children" (1915, 25). "The woman's outlook on life is to save, to care for, to help. Men make wounds," she argued, as Gilman had done in *The Man-Made World*, "and women bind them up" (26).[3] Maternalism thus conceived was not only a matter of women having children and caring for them in the home, but, as Carol Bacchi has pointed out, of their being able to turn the putative impulse to have and to care for those children upon a world that was seen to be in need of such attention (1980, 133) as a result, according to McClung, of "too much masculinity" (1915, 153). This notion was central to the politics of feminism of the first wave, which, Mariana Valverde has shown, while it made a case for women's "political and social rights as a matter of equal justice ... also used utilitarian and organicist arguments that grounded women's cause in an affirmation of their [reproductive] role" (1992, 3).[4] Although "deeply rooted" in what are now regarded by feminists as reductive and biologically determinist notions of gender, the early twentieth-century feminist idea of woman as mother nonetheless took a new view of women's work, seeking simultaneously to expand the limited domestic sphere of mothers and to provide a meaningful role in the world for women without children, unmarried women, and all the "superfluous" women of the mid to late nineteenth century. All women, according to McClung and most first-wave feminists, were "naturally the guardians of the race" (1915, 25).[5] As she put it in *In Times Like*

These, "we see now, it is not so much a woman's duty to bring children into the world, as to see what sort of world she is bringing them into, and what their contribution will be to it" (28).

McClung was criticized throughout the second wave of feminism in Canada for a conservatism with regard to ideologies of gender and maternal feminism that characterizes her writing, as it does more broadly the white and middle-class struggle for suffrage and equal rights for women between the 1880s and the Second World War. Veronica Strong-Boag, in her introduction to the 1972 edition of *In Times Like These*, argues that "McClung did not develop a radical ideology. A mind formed by a Victorian belief system and a Methodist social gospel both of which emphasized the special attributes of women was limited in its freedom to develop" (xx). Wayne Roberts in 1979 suggests that maternal feminism shows women of the period struggling to adapt the push for equality to existing ideological pressures to conform to a domestic and maternal ideal. "It is this adaptation," he writes, "which led to the contradictory nature of maternal feminist aspirations and which accounts for the ultimately disappointing and limited ideological and political gains made by the first self-conscious generation of women's activists in Canadian history" (45). According to Roberts, the maternal feminist figure of "the mother of the race" displaced the earlier feminist incarnation, the "New Woman," and in doing so effectively destroyed the radical potential of first-wave politics. This second-wave view of the first wave now needs revisiting, in part because it is less maternalism *per se* than racialized and classed maternalism that is at stake in current feminist analysis of the period; recent reappraisals of the New Woman and first-wave ideas of motherhood, moreover, have cast new light upon the ideological construction and circulation of these figures.[6]

The New Woman who appeared in the late 1880s was the first public figure in the West to whom the term "feminist" as a politics of individual freedom was popularly attached.[7] She sought "emancipation" from gender-based restrictions; she wanted the vote and higher education and what the later twentieth century valorizes as choice – in partners, marriage, the bearing of children, and work. She would go to school, have a career, smoke, drink, live alone, travel, practise birth control. Her actions, at least as they were configured in contemporary fictional and journalistic representations, were understood to be opposed to motherhood as a defining characteristic of femininity and as a "natural" constraint upon activity and mobility. For "her transgressions," and because she chose "not to pursue the conventional bourgeois woman's career of marriage and motherhood" (1990, 1), Ann Ardis has suggested, the New Woman of the early 1890s was regarded as a social hazard. She was, as Ardis puts it, "accused of instigating the second fall of man" (1) – or, more precisely, the fall of the British Empire, putative apex of civilization.[8] In the imperial framework the New Woman functioned as an index of the problems that generally fell into the category of what Valverde notes was "ambiguously known as 'degeneration'" (1992, 8). By refusing to have children, she failed to increase the population as she should; by taking up hazardous activities, she endangered her ability to bear children and to care for them. The New Woman was thus seen to contribute to – if not to be entirely responsible for – the perceived decline of "the race" that was marked after 1880 by a dropping birth rate, a rising infant mortality rate, and an increase in "racial" diseases such as tuber-culosis. It was also marked by a seeming rise in physical weakness among Britons. The Boer War had proved to be a crisis for the British Empire in part because of the widely noted failure of many recruits to meet military standards.[9] Medical and social discourse of the late nineteenth century bristles with reminders to women of the dangers to their reproductive capacity of too much education, long hours of work, and smoking, drinking, and travel.[10]

The New Woman is seen by late twentieth-century critics such as Roberts to have stood for "individualism" (Ardis 1990, 27) and radical change in gender ideologies. She is also represented in second-wave critiques as a site of conflict for first-wave feminists who wanted liberation but sought a more conservative and thus, for many, arguably more effective means of pursuing it. Many accounts such as Roberts's of the first wave implicitly suggest that the mother of the race appeared on the scene in response to the New Woman, reframing the push for equal rights within the more acceptable ideology of maternalism that emerges so clearly across a broad discursive and representational range in the 1890s. Schreiner and Gilman are early proponents of a discourse of liber-ation and rights based on reproduction as a biological and moral function. Anglo-Australian feminist Louisa Lawson made a similar case in the 1890s for the "advancement" of women as mothers in her woman-produced journal *The Dawn*. Women were morally superior to men, Gilman, Lawson, McClung, and Schreiner all maintained, because they were, as virtually every contemporary discourse told them, mothers. Women as mothers needed more rights and political engagement so they could put their superior morality to work for the good of society as a whole. Society, it was held, needed this feminine engagement if it were to continue to move forward in the great march of progress.[11] The problem that McClung and her contemporaries have thus represented for feminist history is their apparent marking of what is usually seen to have been a *downward* shift from individualist "equal rights feminism" to maternalism. Maternal feminism, from this perspective, shows women returning to the conservative ideologies of gender that the New Woman had rejected.

But maternal feminism, as Misao Dean has demonstrated, is not so clearly divided from New Woman politics (60). Questions of motherhood, reproduction, and biological and social "duty" are certainly what also problematize individualist feminism, at least in the context of British imperial expansionism during these years, when ideologies of motherhood, as Anna Davin suggests, underwent a significant cultural shift. Davin has drawn attention to the ways that conservative notions of motherhood as a duty began to circulate with increased intensity after the 1870s when, as she points out, population became the empire's most pressing issue. In relation to what John Strachey has observed was the largest and most rapid acquisition of territory the British empire had even known, an apparently declining Anglo-Saxon birth rate and rising infant mortality rate after 1880 exacerbated an expansionist anxiety that there would not be enough Britons "to fill the empty spaces of the empire" (Davin 1978, 10).[12] In Canada, eugenist Caleb Saleeby was quoted in *Maclean's* in January 1920 on the potential consequences of a diminishing birth rate at a juncture when "the Peace Treaty adds another million square miles or so to our vast Empire, already famishing for men" (46). This anxiety about the future of the empire can be seen to underpin the construction of the New Woman, an index of decline and a repository for fears about "population and power" (Davin 1978, 9).[13] It is possible to see how this anxiety also produced an imagined antidote in the figure of woman as mother of the race.

If, as Ardis notes, "an enormous amount of polemic" was wielded against the New Woman (1), an even greater amount of propaganda was directed at the mother of the race, glorifying maternalism and endlessly reminding women that their reproduction was vital to the advancement of the empire. The objective of this outpouring in the 1890s was of course to make motherhood both more urgent and more attractive. Maternity was, Davin suggests, "to be given new dignity: it was the duty and destiny of women to be the 'mothers of the race,' but also their great reward" (13). The elevation and glorification of the mother, however, situated women, as Lucy Bland has commented, not "as mothers in general, but as mothers of 'the nation' and of 'the race'" (1995, 70).[14] For this reason, Bland suggests, the "idea of 'Woman as Mother' was mobilized by many feminists. It both empowered women, giving them a vantage point of superiority from which to speak, while simultaneously locating that vantage point within a discourse of racial superiority" (70). That is, when women positioned themselves as mothers of the race, they also became, as Carolyn Burdett indicates, "agents" of empire, progress, and the upward evolutionary climb of "the race" (1998, 48). As Emily Murphy would later put it, women, as mothers, were "called to [their] mission of ruling the world" as never before ("Overpopulation and Birth Control," *Vancouver Sun*, 1 October, 1932, 2).

As Davin has shown and Murphy's comment suggests, the late nineteenth-century ideology of motherhood shifts in the context of rapid territorial growth in terms of evolution and nature, "race" and the "spread" of "civilization." In the 1860s Charles Dilke had characterized the British empire as "Saxondom." Dilke's idea of what J.R. Seeley later called "the expansion of England" was that it was the effect of the "natural" rise of the Anglo-Saxon "race" towards global dominance, a putatively organic movement of Britons and English-speaking peoples into other nations. In the travels he recounts in *Greater Britain*, he carried with him a "conception, however imperfect, of the grandeur of our race, already girdling the earth, which it is destined, perhaps, eventually to overspread" (1869, vii). Dilke's vocabulary implicitly gestures towards social Darwinist and Spencerian theories of the "survival of the fittest" in racialized national categories. By the end of the nineteenth century, empire had come to be configured less as a political and territorial expanse acquired through aggressive militarism than as a matter of the inevitable and eminently desirable evolutionary progress of "Saxondom." As Victoria Tring in Sara Jeannette Duncan's 1906 novel *Set in Authority* puts it, this was no longer the "empire of England" but "the empire of the race" (103).

The value of such a shift to women in a pre-suffrage era is obvious. Women would have clear and meaningful work in an empire (or nation) framed in terms of race if they were configured as the mothers of that race, both as the bearers of its citizens and as the moral superintendents of its future. They could not have such work or value in an empire or a nation framed in terms of military acquisition, government, and bureaucracy.

In many second-wave accounts of the first-wave movement, maternal feminists are seen to have exploited the potential for "advancement" that imperialism as a politics of evolution, population, and race offered them. Bacchi, for instance, maintains that suffragists not only "shared" the conservative ideology of woman's role as mother but also "capitalized on [it] to gain themselves positions of power" (1980, 133).[15] First-wave feminists like McClung, it is implied, only took the position of maternalism because it enabled them to articulate and perform a kind of gynocentric agency that the New Woman represented but had not been able to achieve. In taking this position, however, they are also seen to have doomed first-wave feminism to what critics now regularly note as its failure. With few exceptions, the maternalists' position is understood by post-second-wave feminism to be essentialist and determinist, reductive and limiting; maternalists are seen to be capitulating to patriarchal gender ideology, investing blindly and unquestioningly in the rhetoric of race, empire, and reproduction. Fiamengo has suggested that the late twentieth-century "suspicion" of maternalism is "to some degree historically conditioned, a product of second-wave feminist theorizing, which equates the elevation of motherhood with conservative politics and anti-feminist backlash" (1999–2000, 83). This is an important argument, because it foregrounds the extent to which the New Woman is often represented as a "real" feminist, while the maternalists are seen to be too deeply embedded in patriarchal ideologies of gender to be more than "seemingly feminist" (Dean 1986, 60).

The objectives for both categories were nonetheless fundamentally the same. Individualist New Women and maternal feminists both wanted equal rights, suffrage, education, and a range of social reforms that would counter gender-based discrimination. First-wave maternal feminists did not themselves indicate any consciousness of a shift or a contradiction: they did not see themselves as *not* New Women. In fact, by 1921, when McClung published her suffrage novel, *Purple Springs*, the ideal maternal feminist – her heroine Pearlie Watson – *was* "the New Woman" (111). For later twentieth-century feminism, the motherly Pearl is a problematic New Woman, a maternalist who is only disguised as a "real" feminist, a mother of the race who has appropriated the feminist designation with the object of re-implementing conservative ideologies of gender. She encodes a capitulation and a retroactive movement to biological essentialism. For McClung, however, there is no apparent contradiction between Pearl's New Woman designation and that of her predecessors.[16] In McClung's view, Pearl is a radical and subversive agent of change and progress, a builder of nation and empire, a feminist messiah for the imagined New World.

The tension between mothering and liberation was not new to maternal feminism. It had always been a problem in individualist New Woman politics, since throughout the 1880s and '90s the population and expansion questions had been so prominent in imperial thinking. W.T. Stead made the point in 1894 in an article on "The Novel of the Modern Woman" that the "modern" feminist argument that woman has a mind "in no wise involves or implies any forgetting of her sex, of her destiny, and of her duty as the mother of the race. So far from this being the case, it will be seen that in almost every case the novels of the modern woman are pre-occupied with questions of sex, questions of marriage, questions of maternity" (65).

Misao Dean has similarly suggested that feminist fiction in Canada during the heyday of the New Woman conveys a profound concern with both "personal autonomy" and "maternal self-sacrifice." Many New Woman novels in Canada "undertake to overcome that split, to explain it and render it invisible. These novels resignify women's struggle to define a new kind of 'self' as consistent with their newly biologically circumscribed roles as mothers of the race, and in so doing suggest that the New Woman is really the old woman after all. Despite intermittent, seemingly feminist elements, these texts are deeply and fundamentally conservative, even in their assertion of women's sexual desire, personal autonomy, and dissatisfaction with the social institutions of marriage and motherhood" (60). This "split" is certainly perceptible in English-Canada's best-known New Woman novels, Joanna Wood's *The Untempered Wind* (1894), Sara Jeannette Duncan's *A Daughter of Today* (1894),

Maria Amelia Fytche's *Kerchiefs to Hunt Souls* (1895), and Lily Dougall's *The Madonna of a Day* (1895).

What Stead and Dean both indicate is that the mother of the race was not less radical than the New Woman, and not really all that different. What *was* different was the argument that women would be "advanced" not for their own sake or even, as Louisa Lawson and her 1890s contemporaries suggested in *The Dawn*, to mark a putative level of civilization in a given national or imperial category. Instead their "advancement" would enable them, as McClung put it, effectively "to serve and save the race." It was the perception of the condition of the empire that had shifted. Maternal feminism emerged as the dominant discourse of women's rights not because women saw an opportunity in shifting imperialism and took it but because they were themselves a part of that shift. That is, first-wave maternalism is not a gendered inflection of a masculine idea of empire: it is imperialism itself.

By the turn of the century, imperialists everywhere – conservatives, radicals, right-leaning, left-leaning, anti-feminists and feminists, eugenists and environmentalists – all put new faith in the regenerative work of maternalism. The pervasiveness of the idea of woman as the mother of the race in the imperial context shows it to have been broadly culturally internalized across gender and class categories. On all sides of the period's various debates about science, politics, race, gender, and empire, "one conclusion remained the same," as Bacchi notes: "woman's chief duty lay in the breeding and care of new citizens" (1980, 139). The identification of maternal feminists as mothers of the race is thus not so much political as ideological. Feminist discourse of this period emerges in lockstep with that of race regeneration not simply because regenerationist ideas offered a way out of gender inequality. The prospect of imperial conquest by other nations was as pervasive and deeply rooted as Cold War anxieties would be for North Americans in the decades after the Second World War; in the imperial contest, women were "the white hope" (McClung 1945, 182). What was at stake was perceived as the social good; what they worked for was not individual good but the good of "the race." According to McClung, "women *must* work, if the race will survive" (1915, 101, my emphasis). The "adaptation" which Roberts notes is comprehensible then less as a capitulation to anti-feminist ideas of womanhood than as a cultural shift within the context of shifting imperialism and imperial expansionism, from the politics of individualism associated with the New Woman in the 1880s and '90s to the early twentieth-century notions of women's liberation as a matter of social rather than individual good.

The discourse of race regeneration that began to circulate with such intensity in the 1880s and that underpins the emergence of the New Woman and the mother of the race was not itself fundamentally "feminist," despite its glorification of maternalism. Indeed, quite the opposite was true. But the feminist mother of the race *was* subversive. Her goal was to implement radical social change that began with the liberation of women. First-wave feminists responded, as did most women, to the period's rhetoric of motherhood and race regeneration, but they (New Women *and* maternal feminists) also made this rhetoric yield to the imperatives of gender equality – political, social, material, economic – that not all women sought. They redirected, in effect, the imperial shift to elevated ideas of motherhood away from a domestic and reproductive imperative to the ideas of maternal professionalization and agency (motherhood as a career, maternalism as a subject position) that continue at the beginning of the twenty-first century to represent a significant aspect of gender ideology and feminist debate in the West.

For second-wave feminism, the preoccupation with "questions of maternity" is the central problem of first-wave feminism. While it still figures in the third wave in arguments such as Dean's, the basis for feminist dissociation, in Canada at any rate, from figures such as McClung and Murphy, as Grant-Cummings's earlier-cited comment indicates, is the investment of "questions of maternity" in ideas of race.[17] If imperialism is the locus for the emergence of a radical politics of maternal feminism, it is also the central problem for the late twentieth century and early twenty-first critique of the first wave. It is not so much that women took up motherhood as a position "from which to speak" (Bland 1995, 70) but that maternal feminists were imperialists. Their idea of motherhood was not only reductive and essentialist and (in second-wave terms) "conservative"; it was also embedded in a politics of nation- and empire-building, of racial difference and, inevitably, racial superiority and eugenics.

The engagement of first-wave feminism with the ideas of eugenics has been discussed and compellingly problematized in a number of important studies. Lucy Bland's 1995 *Banishing the Beast: Sexuality and the Early Feminists* is certainly the most influential recent account. Carolyn Burdettt's discussion in "The Hidden Romance of Sexual Science: Eugenics, the Nation and the Making of Modern Feminism" (1998) of Karl Pearson's work is extremely useful. In Canadian history, Angus McLaren's *Our Own Master Race: Eugenics in Canada* (1990) has become a key text in studies of early twentieth-century culture and sexuality, as have Mariana Valverde's *The Age of Light, Soap, and Water: Moral Reform in English Canada, 1885–1925* (1991); Catherine Cleverdon's early study, *The Woman Suffrage Movement in Canada* (1950, 1974); Carol Lee Bacchi's, *Liberation Deferred? The Ideas of the English-Canadian Suffragists, 1877–1918* (1983); and Valverde's critique of the first wave, "When the Mother of the Race Is Free," in the 1992 collection *Gender Conflicts*. The "ambivalence" attending the popular perception of McClung in Canada indicates that the "contradictions" in the first-wave feminist support of eugenics persist. The problem highlighted by these studies, however, is not so much how feminism got to be so maternal but how the idea of maternalism got to be so eugenic – how the anti-feminist principles of "selective breeding" came to be, as one commentator put it, "one with the Woman Question" (Ellis 1914, 46).

2

"Motherhood on the Eugenic Basis"

How the Anti-Feminist Principles of Selective Breeding Became "One with the Woman Question"

The mark of the following pages is that they assume the principle of what we may call Eugenic Feminism ... There is immediate need for the presentation of a case which is, from first to last, and at whatever cost, eugenic; but which also – or, rather, therefore – makes the highest claims on behalf of woman and womanhood, so that indeed, in striving to demonstrate the vast importance of the woman question for the composition of the coming race, I may claim to be much more feminist than the feminists.

Saleeby 1911, *Woman and Womanhood*

First-wave feminism such as is articulated in McClung's *In Times Like These* was maternal as it was built around the figure of the mother (Stong-Boag 1972, viii). Maternalism, or the cultural situating of women's subjectivity in motherhood, is not definitively or necessarily eugenic, but first-wave maternal feminism, as the explicit qualification of the figure of the mother *of the race* indicates, certainly was. Its first concern was with the preservation of the globally dispersed white Anglo-Saxon community through a collective addressing of what was seen to be preventing "good" racial stock from being born and maintained. Like that of Schreiner and Gilman, McClung's writing was embedded in eugenical principles. War was bad because it was dysgenic, decimating good racial stock and leaving the "unfit" to reproduce. Alcohol was dangerous because it was a "racial poison." Careless unions between "unfit" men and women were to be avoided to prevent the production of children "who are a burden and a menace to society" (1915, 138–9). Women were mothers of the race who would not only have children but would save Anglo-Saxondom from decline by altering the conditions under which those children would be born.

Works such as *In Times Like These* indicate just how thoroughly the dominant voice of feminism in the British Empire came to be aligned with the project of preserving and improving "the race." In other words, they show how powerfully maternal feminism came to be, as Saleeby suggested of motherhood, "harnessed to the service of eugenics" (1909, xiv). By 1915, when McClung published her suffrage manifesto, the feminist project in eugenics and the eugenic project in feminism are so discursively entangled that they are difficult to separate. This convergence is problematic not only because it marks first-wave feminism's investment in ideas of racial superiority and imperial dominance but because, as I have suggested, this investment is itself ideological. Feminists, as Carolyn Burdett has shown, were "called" by the discourse of eugenics, and their response was partly a matter of conscious self-representation and endorsement of articulated cultural values and norms and partly a process of recognition that does not take place consciously. That such a process – of what Louis Althusser has called "interpellation" or (mis)recognition as a subject in response to external cultural pressures – *did* take place is evident, both in the increased support for eugenical legislation and ideas by increasingly influential feminists such as McClung and Murphy and in the extent to which eugenists who were not feminists first sought to align their objectives with those of the struggle for gender equality.

Eugenics had emerged in 1883, when Francis Galton gave the name to what he had been developing since the 1860s as a science of improving breeding stock in all life forms, including – especially – humans. "Ability" in humans, Galton had argued in his 1869 book, *Hereditary Genius*, was inherited, passing specifically from father to son, primarily among the upper classes. The transmission of "genius" could be seen, he maintained, in the extent to which particular qualities appeared in successive generations of these classes. Galton's theories, Burdett has noted, "had been facilitated by the publication in 1859 of *Origin of Species* by his cousin, Charles Darwin" as well as "by Herbert Spencer's ideas about social competition" (1998, 46) and the survival of the fittest. "Ability" was not for Galton an effect of social privilege but rather an inherent quality that served as an index of a superior evolutionary status. The British upper classes whose qualities he charted had risen to their rank naturally, he suggested, because of their particular hereditary qualities. They were, in Spencer's terminology, the fittest representatives of what the global expansion of the British Empire had shown to be the fittest "race." Eugenics was thus concerned (perversely, perhaps, given its origins in theories of evolution and natural selection) with the protection and promotion of a national and ethnic category of the fittest – what would be designated "*the* race" – through the control of reproduction. "Judicious mating" was its first premise, not only to maintain the existing qualities of the middle and upper classes but to foster "all influences that tend in however remote a degree to give to the suitable races or strains of blood a better chance of prevailing speedily over the less suitable than they otherwise would have had" (Galton, cited in Burdett 1998, 46).

Eugenics took two different approaches to the "problem" of "judicious mating." On the one hand, it addressed questions of "breeding in" solid genetic qualities: this was known as "positive eugenics." On the other hand, it undertook to "breed out" those characteristics, thought to be genetically transmitted, that might be seen to pollute the gene pool or the "stock" from which "the race" was reproduced: this was "negative eugenics." "Positive" characteristics would remain embedded in the period's constructed social and evolutionary hierarchies of class and race. The upper and middle classes were seen to possess "ability"; European national categories were configured as more evolved than non-European.

"Negative" characteristics were similarly based on class and race and were presented as "tendencies" – to ill health, mental illness, alcoholism, tuberculosis. Eugenics thus addressed social problems in terms of individuals as members of predetermined categories; it undertook a "scientific" explanation of the effects of the economic and imperial structures that themselves constituted and insistently reinforced categories of class and race. The "poor" were sickly because they were genetically inferior. Non-Europeans were in need of "uplift" because they were not racially "advanced." In effect, eugenics was a discourse and a technology of empire; it explained racial and social differences and provided a "scientific" justification for imperialism. It also provided a framework within which to mark and affirm gender difference and to legislate the reproductive work of women.

Since it had always been concerned first with increasing and improving "stock" through controlled reproduction in which women were to be marshalled as breeders, women had always been, in one sense, at the centre of eugenics. They were, as Bland puts it, "the main objects of intervention" (1995, 232) for eugenists and the primary focus of eugenist rhetoric. There was not much that was feminist about early eugenics, however. In Galton's earliest theories of "Hereditary Genius," women were positioned as little more than vehicles for the transmission of particular qualities between father and son; what he called "genius" passed between men.[18] For Galton there could not be female agency in the process of selection. Women were acted upon rather than acting. According to Galtonian eugenics, if women were to assist in what really mattered – the advancement of the race – they could only do so by accepting a biologically determined subordination to men, rationalized by their perceived function as breeders and attended by numerous restrictions upon their mobility and their intellectual pursuits. Galton, as Saleeby noted in 1911, "lent his name to the anti-suffrage side," mainly to discourage women from activities that could affect their ability to reproduce. These activities were dishearteningly numerous. "Mainline eugenicists" opposed higher education for women because, "so the reasoning went, [it] diverted women's biological energy from the task of reproduction to the burdens of intellectual or worldly activities" (Kevles 1985, 89). For the same reasons, women (or middle-class women at least), were not to work, or, indeed, to undertake *any* activity that was not aimed at healthy reproduction. It is thus not surprising that, as Saleeby blandly noted early, "the feminists, one and all, so far as Anglo-Saxondom is concerned ... are either unaware of the meaning of eugenics at all, or are up in arms at once when the eugenist – or at any rate this eugenist, who is a male person – mildly inquires: But what about motherhood?" (1911, 7–8).

As Saleeby's comment suggests, feminists of the late 1880s and '90s did not necessarily see in eugenics the way out of gender-based inequality. But, although Galton's idea of motherhood could not seem particularly liberating, prominent eugenists were already working to change the way women were called to eugenics. As early as 1885, only a couple of years after Galton had first identified his science, his protégé Karl Pearson had attempted to draw the emergent public discourse of women's rights and that of the empire's reproductive needs into a working union through the inaugural paper for his discussion group, the Men and Women's Club.[19] Pearson undertook to include women in what he saw as a national project of eugenical overhaul, foregrounding the centrality of the work of reproduction that was to be the route to strengthening the nation as an expansionist force. For eugenists like Pearson, Burdett observes, the nation was at the centre of eugenics (1998, 48), and women, as the bearers of the next generation, "were the key to national progress" (52).

While Pearson did not see a future in which women were *not* primarily mothers, by representing women as intelligent and voluntary agents of regeneration (53), he significantly framed the Woman Question as one that was not opposed to but was profoundly connected with the questions of eugenics. Saleeby (who, despite his claims, was certainly not a feminist) later took the position that "the very first thing that the feminist movement must prove is that it is eugenic. If it be so, its claims are unchallengeable; if it be what may contrariwise be called *dysgenic*, no arguments in its favour are of any avail" (1911, 6). As he indicates in his appeal to women's rights activists, eugenics also had to prove that it was feminist if it was to have any influence upon what he, like other eugenists, represented as the most important figures in the work of empire.

"It is no exaggeration," eugenist Mary Scharlieb wrote in 1912, "to say that on woman depends the welfare of the race ... It is merely a truism that the race will be whatever the women of the race make it" (5).[20] Havelock Ellis, probably the best-known and most influential writer in English on matters of eugenics and what he called "social hygiene" in the early century, would intensify this claim, suggesting in 1914 that on feminism, or the woman movement itself, depended the success of the eugenical project and thus of the progress of the nation and of the empire. "The breeding of men lies largely in the hands of women," wrote Ellis. "That is why the question of Eugenics is to a great extent one with the woman question. The realization of Eugenics in our social life can only be attained with the realization of the woman movement in its latest and completest phase as an enlightened culture of motherhood, in all that motherhood involves alike on the physical and the psychic sides" (46). For Ellis, feminism was – or ought to be – actually leading the race upward. It was, he intimated, the single most important factor in the "realization of eugenics," and the sooner eugenists and feminists both came to this realization, the better for everyone.

In the context of eugenics, Ellis implied, feminists did not need to struggle for recognition of their political equality and special biological difference understood as moral superiority. Eugenics now in the early twentieth century was onside in the great fight for the Women's Cause. It saw that suffrage was leading "the race" forward; it saw the necessity of female enfranchisement for, as feminists argued, social and imperial "advancement." Eugenists were explicit and often blunt in articulating this position. LaReine Helen Baker made this claim in 1912 in *Race Improvement and Eugenics: A Little Book on a Great Subject*: "At present, Eugenics views the feminist movement from the point of view of political power as a means to national efficiency ... This standpoint is the more natural because there is every reason to believe that while the objective of the feminist is nominally Votes for Women it is actually an assertion of woman's all-round equality with men" (86).

Saleeby was even more direct: "I believe in the vote because I believe it will be eugenic, will reform the conditions of marriage and divorce in the eugenic sense, and will serve the cause of what I have elsewhere called 'preventive eugenics,' which strives to protect healthy stocks from the 'racial poisons,' such as venereal disease, alcohol, and, in a relatively infinitesimal degree, lead" (1911, 24). Saleeby concurred with Baker that "It is to the interest of all who do not take a sex-party view of citizenship, to abbreviate this struggle" (Baker, 87) – not, notably, for the purposes of individual liberty for women but for the good of the race and "national efficiency."

Ellis would make a similar statement in 1914: "The attainment of the suffrage if it is a beginning and not an end, will ... have a real and positive value in liberating the woman's movement from a narrow and sterilizing phase of its course" (86). The ballot, Ellis held, quoting American suffragist Elizabeth Cady Stanton, was "at most, only the vestibule to women's emancipation" (85) and therefore only a means to what was presented in eugenical discourse as the *real* end of feminism: the preservation of the race. Ellis's point of view in 1914 was that women should be released from the exhausting distractions of the struggle for the vote and empowered to undertake and protect their work of mothering, crucial to "national efficiency."

For eugenists like Saleeby, the crux of the problem that feminism presented to the eugenic project inhered not in the politics of individual emancipation and collective resistance to reproduction (although these are almost certainly what underpin their anxiety) but in the concentration of white, educated, middle-class women within the ranks of organized feminism. For most eugenists, it was the middle classes who were suffering a drop in the birth rate; Saleeby at any rate noted no comparable drop in the birth rate of the lower classes, only an alarming increase in "inferior" stock. It was easy to pinpoint the apparent defection of middle-class women as the explanation for this seeming decline. These women, Saleeby suggested, were "increasingly to be found enlisted in the ranks of Feminism, and fighting the great fight for the Women's Cause" (1911, 14).

"The belief that feminism actually posed a danger to the eugenics movement was shared by many of its adherents" (1990, 21), McLaren notes, primarily because these women were also to be the mothers of future generations. "If our modern knowledge of heredity is to be admitted at all," Saleeby argued, "it follows that the choice of women for motherhood is of the utmost moment for the future of mankind" (1911, 5). In other words, it was not just any women who were "called" to national and imperial duty. The "principle beside which all others are trivial, [is] that *the best women must be the mothers of the future*" (6), Saleeby maintained. Eugenist authors William C.D. and Catherine D. Whetham would frame this sentiment even more dramatically in their 1909 book, *The Family and the Nation: A Study in Natural Inheritance and Social Responsibility*: "Woe to the nation whose best women refuse their natural and most glorious burden!" (199).

In a similar gesture, Ellis would make an appeal in *The Task of Social Hygiene* (1914) to this category of "best" women as the most valuable progenitors of an improved "race." "Motherhood on the eugenic basis," he wrote, "is a deliberate and selective process, calling for the highest intelligence as well as the finest emotional and moral aptitudes, so that all the best energies of a long evolution of womanhood in the paths of modern culture here find their final outlet. The breeding of children further involves the training of children, and since the expansion of Social Hygiene renders education a far larger and more delicate task than it has ever been before, the responsibilities laid upon women by the evolution of civilization become correspondingly great" (46–7).

The idea that evolutionary superiority was marked in class as well as race had been a founding principle of Galton's eugenics; his *Hereditary Genius* traced "ability" in British men of the middle and upper classes, seeing social status as an index of natural rank. Feminism "on the eugenic basis" likewise built upon the conception of a superior rank of women. Those who were interpellated by the feminist and eugenist call to duty were to recognize themselves as the most highly evolved creatures of the most highly evolved race, intelligent, educated, morally superior, naturally selected to reproduce, and currently engaged in the struggle for equality with men through woman suffrage.

When Saleeby gestured at Galton's anti-feminism, and argued, as Ellis would too, that the choice of women for motherhood was of the utmost moment, he directed his rhetoric at the educated white, middle-class women who, he maintained, were "increasingly deserting the ranks of motherhood and leaving the blood of inferior women to constitute half of all future generations" (1911, 14). What was imperative was convincing these women of "the unchangeable and beneficent facts of biology ... so that they and those of their sisters who are of the same natural rank ... shall ... furnish an ever-increasing proportion of our wives and mothers, to the great gain of themselves, and of men, and of the future" (14). Indeed, he argued more compellingly, "the leading women who in any way countenance such measures as deprive the blood of the future of its due contribution from the best women of the present, are leading not only one sex but the race as a whole to ruin" (5). Feminism, in other words, would remain a primary cause of the decline that was seen to be besetting Anglo-Saxondom (it would be "dysgenic") until the "best women," whom Saleeby identified *as* feminists, took up motherhood as the guiding principle of the politics of women's advancement. For Saleeby, this was the first principle of what he called "Eugenic Feminism" (7).

Valverde has pointed out that in first-wave feminist commentary, "the ethnocentric social construction of womanhood as moral teacher left no doubt about which women were most suited to lead feminism as well as world progress" (1992, 10). Ellis's case for "an enlightened culture of motherhood" indicates that what Saleeby called Eugenic Feminism was a discourse within which white, middle-class, Anglo-Saxon women could constitute themselves as national – racialized – subjects in superior relation not only to the women (and men) of other nations but to other categories of national womanhood such as indigenous, working-class, and immigrant women. Eugenic feminists, the "enlightened culture of motherhood"

promoted by Saleeby and Ellis, could take charge of the crucial
aspects of race regeneration both through what Galton had defined
as positive eugenics and through negative eugenics, using a range
of measures from birth control to the sexual sterilization of the
putatively unfit. Valued as imperial mothers and bearers of future
improved generations, these women were also characterized, like
Galton's and, later, Ellis's British "men of genius," by a racially
determined and class-specific ability which they were called upon
to put to work not only for the good of their own children but for
"the race" at large. A primary aspect of this work for middle-class
women was the instruction of "unenlightened" mothers, the "educational strategy" that Bland has identified as central to the work
of making fit mothers and better children (1995, 232), and that
emerged under the name of "mothercraft."

The term "mothercraft" came into circulation in the first decade
of the twentieth century in relation to the work of Dr Sykes, medical
officer of health for St Pancras and a London-based organizer of
maternally focused education strategies (Davin 1978, 39). Sykes is
noteworthy for his work to institutionalize the training of mothers
and thus to establish a national apparatus that functioned to incul-
cate women into an ideology of eugenic maternalism. His Schools
for Mothers were seen to offer crucial guidance to poor and working-
class women. Those providing the guidance were largely "members
of the upper and middle classes who found it a worthy (and perhaps
a fashionable) cause," and who undertook the dissemination of
advice on issues such as breast-feeding, bottle-feeding, domestic
hygiene, food preparation, making babies' clothes, baby care, and
– importantly – the care of the mother herself (Davin 1978, 39).
The St Pancras centre also provided dinners for mothers and took
the position that "one of the first steps needed to effect the political
and social emancipation of women is a crusade on the part of man
calling upon her to eat. And there can never be a really strong race
of Britons until she does" (Dora Bunting, cited in Davin 1978, 40).
Mothercraft, this comment indicates, had two goals. One was to
protect all mothers, the other was to make "better" babies. It had,
moreover, another effect. It provided a location for women to go
to work for the good of the nation and to perform their "motherly"
work outside the home.

Although Sykes's St Pancras undertaking sought first to help what
were constructed as disadvantaged and ignorant mothers of the

"lower" classes through the intervention of educated women from the "upper" classes, the ideas of mothercraft turned out to have a pervasive appeal across British imperial culture and throughout the empire. In 1914, Ellis observed that the Schools for Mothers introduced in 1907 "are now spreading everywhere. In the end they will probably be considered necessary centres for any national system of puericulture. Every girl at the end of her school life should be expected to pass through a certain course of training at a School for Mothers. It would be the technical school for the working-class mother, while such a course would be invaluable for any girl, whatever her social class, even if she is never called to be a mother herself or to have the care of children" (9–10). The nation, in other words, depended on the production of a stock of healthy women across class boundaries, trained in the "necessary" work of bearing and raising children, and ready at any point to be "called" to work on behalf of the state and "the race." Mothercraft thus marks the institutionalization in the first decade of the twentieth century of eugenist ideas about women and women's reproduction and social work, and the basis for the later twentieth-century professionalization of motherhood.

Middle-class feminists such as McClung who took up the rhetoric of advancing women in order "to go forward as a race" looked for ways to implement the politics of eugenic motherhood through the apparatus of mothercraft. *In Times Like These* pays considerable attention to the problem of "male moralists [who] have cried out for large families" (1915, 139), noting both a reduced vitality and strength in children and adverse effects upon women called to reproduce in great numbers in the expansionist years. The children might be "anemic and rickety, ill-nourished and deformed" while the "mothers, already overburdened and underfed, die in giving them birth" (139). McClung maintained that what was needed was not more children but "better children, and a higher value set upon all human life" (141). "Thinking women," she suggested, recognized "that population is very desirable," especially in the "Far West" of Canada, where, for McClung, the birth rate was seen to be as much in decline as in the imperial centre and the need to fill up the spaces of empire was immediate and urgent. But they also saw that "more care should be exerted for the protection of the children who are already here" (140), as well as for their mothers.

"Thousands of babies die every year from preventable causes," McClung wrote. "Free milk depositories and district nurses and free dispensaries would save many of them. In the Far West, on the border of civilization, where women are beyond the reach of nurses and doctors, many mothers and babies die every year. How would it be to try to save them? Delegations of public-spirited women have waited upon august bodies of men, and pleaded the cause of these brave women who are paying the toll of colonization, and have asked that Government nurses be sent to them in their hour of need. But up to date not one dollar of Government money has been spent on them" (140–1).

It was, according to McClung, women who would change all this. Women themselves – or, at least, middle-class, nationally identified women – would legislate their own and other women's reproduction and the circumstances within which it occurred. Invoking some of the measures undertaken in Germany in the early years of the century, she described the work of controlled reproduction as a matter of protecting women and children: "It is interesting to note what the Germans do to conserve their population. Germany has three societies whose work it is to conserve the race: (1) The Repopulation Society, (2) The League for the Protection of Motherhood, (3) The League for Infant Protection. Every woman who gives birth to a child is given a six weeks' rest by virtue of Government insurance. The motto of the League for the Protection of Motherhood is *No mother shall bear her child in anxiety or need*" (*Maclean's*, July 1916, 38). In other words, it was less women's duty to reproduce than the duty of the state to protect them in reproduction and, crucially, after it, not as martyrs to the cause of empire but citizens supported in their work for the common good.

Eugenic feminists like McClung would always acknowledge reproduction as a duty, but as only one of the particular duties of the "enlightened," and as something that did not preclude other engagements with the work of nation- and empire-building. "Every mother had two duties to her home, one was to train her children to be good citizens of the world and the other was to try and make the world a fit place for her children to live in" (*Winnipeg Tribune*, 6 July 1914, PABC). The first duty was easier to comprehend; as far as McClung was concerned, it was the second duty that presented a major challenge to women, and the defining of that second duty that was the most pressing task for feminists. In this McClung departed slightly from the kind of emphasis on reproduction that is apparent in Gilman's 1898 *Women and Economics*. In her preface Gilman indicated that she wanted the book "to reach in especial the thinking women of to-day, and urge upon them a new sense, not only of their social responsibility as individuals, but of their measureless racial importance as makers of men" (1898, reprint 1966, xxxix). McClung undertook the same work, but wanted to urge upon thinking women first their social responsibility to "the race," not as "makers of men" only but as agents of social organization and management.

In the second volume of her autobiography McClung would explain her investment in the Woman's Christian Temperance Union (WCTU) thus: "Women must be made to feel their responsibility. All this protective love, this instinctive mother love, must be organized in some way, and made effective. There was enough of it in the world to do away with all the evils which war upon childhood, undernourishment, slum conditions, child labor, drunkenness. Women could abolish these if they wanted to" (1945, 27). As Strong-Boag has suggested, this passage serves as a statement of purpose for all of McClung's feminism (viii), as it built around the idea of "instinctively" maternal women and undertook to organize that instinct into a massive movement for change.

This was how, moreover, McClung saw women's organizations serving their purpose to humanity. The first cause of women's clubs of any kind was, implicitly, the focusing and effective distribution of "mother-love" (1908, 38), the mobilization of the maternal instinct that made women "naturally the guardians of the race" (1915, 25). "The mother's kindly counsel is the best, I know," she affirmed, "but you cannot always rely upon its being there" (1915, 133). What was needed to supplement the untrained mother was the mobilization of what she called "the last reserves" in the war against degeneration. These were not only the women working "in the department of social welfare, paid by the school board," and not only nurses, teachers and "matron[s] of the Refuge for Unfortunate Women" (132). They were an "army" of unpaid volunteers who "banded together for mutual improvement and social welfare" in organizations that were simultaneously to empower women to "clean ... up things" and to assure them of the value of their maternal work not only at home but beyond the home. "If women could be made to think," McClung suggested in *In Times Like These*, "they would see that it is woman's place to lift high the standard of morality" (43). Making women think and defining the way that "motherly" women could "shape the thought of the world" was the aim of her 1915 suffrage manifesto; that is, its first work was to appeal to the middle-class, Anglo-Saxon, and Christian women who had been identified by eugenical discourse as the linchpins of empire and the only possible saviours of the race.

In a speech delivered around the end of World War I, McClung made the point that progress and the advancement of empire and nation depended on the involvement of women as agents of social change:

There must be other avenues opened for women's activities, if we are to go forward as a race. Many women have already found the way, and are happily pursuing it. They use their leisure to supervise the children's play and study; they read and study, play games and help in various societies, church circles and others, making themselves better companions for their husbands and children. They take time to be happy, healthy and useful. To them, the meaning of life is clear. With that fine type of womanhood, which happily we see very often, we have no concern. They need no word of advice. They are big spokes in the wheels of progress, and mighty factors in shaping the thought of the world. ("Woman's Place in the Band-Wagon")

"They" – eugenic, feminist – are also implicitly called upon here to give a "word of advice" to those women who have not found a "place in the band-wagon" of what is represented in this speech as the inevitable narrative of social "progress" that underpins imperialism.

By the time McClung moved to the forefront of the suffrage movement in Canada, feminism and eugenics shared an ideological basis in the context of imperialism. Both were concerned with liberating women "to serve and save the race" and with creating "an enlightened culture of motherhood" devoted to the imperial mission of ruling the world. Like Gilman's *The Man-Made World* and Schreiner's *Woman and Labour*, *In Times Like These* is a document of what Saleeby called Eugenic Feminism because it reproduced an idea of empowered maternalism that was embedded in racial and social hierarchies.

Saleeby's notion of Eugenic Feminism conflicted with the practical realization of women's rights in a number of compelling ways. Although he situated himself in support of the vote, he also argued in *Woman and Womanhood*, as McLaren has observed, "the 'dysgenic consequences' of women's education, the 'intolerable evil' of married women's work, and the high rate of *male* infant mortality, which he referred to as 'infanticide'" (McLaren 1990, 22–3). That is, his Eugenic Feminism was at least partly a deceptive rhetorical strategy seeking to draw middle-class women's rights activists *back* to home and duty, albeit with the vote and a markedly increased cultural value as progenitors of future generations. Nonetheless, eugenical discourse like Saleeby's provided feminists with an unassailable subject position with a national imperative, and many feminists took it. The eugenic solution was contingent upon the social recognition of a particular ability in white, middle-class women: it was *because* middle-class women were mothers of the race that they were called upon to do so much; it was *because* of the maternal instinct that eugenists had maintained was so powerful that women, as McClung put it, were "spiritually more aware than men," and so necessary, according to Ellis, to the "realization of eugenics." When they thus participated in the discursive construction of the mother of the race, eugenists had in effect accomplished what they indicated they wanted, but probably did not want. Perversely, that is, the discourse of eugenics actually facilitated a much greater expansion of women's work in the public sphere than it had arguably undertaken to promote. First-wave maternal feminism, for its part, was engaged in a much more aggressive nationalist and imperialist push for political power as a means to "efficiency" than it is usually credited with undertaking.

3

Locating McClung's Eugenic Feminism
Didactic Fiction and Racial Education

In this day of war, when men are counted of less value than cattle, it is
a doubtful favor to the child to bring it into life under any circumstances, but to bring children into the world, suffering from the handi-
caps caused by the ignorance, poverty, or criminality of the parents, is
an appalling crime against the innocent and helpless, and yet one about
which practically nothing is said. Marriage, homemaking, and the rearing of children are left entirely to chance, and so it is no wonder that
humanity produces so many specimens who, if they were silk stockings
or boots, would be marked "Seconds."

McClung, *In Times Like These*

Leilani Muir's successful suit against the Alberta government for
wrongful sterilization resulted in the familiarization of most English-
Canadians with the involvement of first-wave feminists in eugenical
legislation in Alberta in the 1920s, so that many readily associate
Nellie McClung, like Emily Murphy, with the 1928 Sexual Sterilization Bill. Murphy, as is now well known, was a leading figure in the
push for eugenical legislation. She wrote extensively in favour of
eugenics and sexual sterilization (her series of articles for the *Vancouver
Sun* in 1932 is usually cited). She also figured prominently in the
early days of the Canadian Committee of Mental Hygiene, the group
formed to address matters pertinent to the containment of the mentally ill, largely through eugenical measures limiting reproduction.

McClung too wrote in support of eugenical principles: first in *In
Times Like These*, obliquely throughout her life in her purity activism
to "serve and save the race," and explicitly in her autobiography.

But her precise involvement in the legislation has been less well documented.[21] She had been nominated by Murphy around 1915 as one of the Alberta members of the Canadian Committee of Mental Hygiene prior to the passage of the Sexual Sterilization Bill. In a 1925 letter to Alberta Minister of Health George Hoadley, Murphy included McClung in her representation of the committee as "persons who were studying the subject closely, and who might fairly be depended upon to take a reasonable stand on matters relating to mental hygiene" (Murphy to Hoadley, 20 April, 1925). It is evident in this letter that McClung was sufficiently supportive in 1925 to be endorsed as a member of "an Advisory Committee ... appointed by the Government for the Gaols and Mental Hospitals ... with full powers to inspect these Institutions, and to report their findings." Her support would have been known by more English-Canadians than just Murphy: McClung had written on eugenics in 1919 in the Toronto magazine *Everywoman's World*. This short article is directed specifically to women ("Listen – Ladies!") and reiterates some of the ground she covered in *In Times Like These*, with eugenics made explicit as the basis for the reforms for which she is arguing:

Another thought which re-occurs and sticks around waiting for some one to explain it – is that marriage, home-making and the rearing of children, are the most haphazard undertakings in our social life. They are undertaken lightly and without preparation. When people raise chickens, they measure the coop and find out how many cubic feet of air each fowl requires, and also figure out, on the hen-house door, what the feed will cost. These considerations determine the size of the flock. No sensible poultry-man will raise more chickens than he can feed! AND yet –

Oh, well, perhaps when there are as many bulletins issued from the Department of Human Welfare as there are now from the Live Stock Department, people will understand more about the science of Eugenics. (*Everywoman's World*, June 1919, 18)

Although McClung does not refer here to specific eugenical legislation, her support of the *ideas* of what she calls "the science of Eugenics" is clear. So, implicitly, is her support for the social measures that could be and in many locations were implemented to attempt to control reproduction in terms of the numbers or quantity as well as perceived quality of the "flock."

McClung's position in the 1920s with regard to the Sexual Sterilization Bill is articulated in *The Stream Runs Fast*, the 1945 volume of her autobiography. This section is frequently cited as evidence of her campaign for eugenics in Alberta. It was, she wrote, "thanks to the foresight and courage" of then provincial Minister of Health George Hoadley that "Alberta had the first Act authorizing the sterilization of the unfit in the British Empire":

Mental deficiency in the schools had increased from one to three per cent, and this seemed to be one measure of prevention. There was fanatical opposition from certain religious bodies, but, I am glad to say that our Opposition Party [the Liberals] gave it our support. I saw the working out of this measure soon after it became law when a poor distracted mother from southern Alberta came to see me, bringing her eighteen-year old daughter who was not quite normal. She was, unfortunately for herself, rather an attractive girl and eager for life at all costs. She had never been able to get past Grade Three in school, but she was as strong as a horse and as good as a man in the harvest field. Her mother was naturally fearful for her safety. (177)

The mother indicates to McClung her concern that Katie will marry "a man ten years older" who is "not quite right either": she would, she maintains, "rather see her dead" (178).

If it is the safety of the young girl for which the mother is fearful, it is the safety of "the race" which has McClung's concern. While she sympathizes with the mother's sense that Katie herself "deserves our protection," what motivates her to get "in touch with one of the Doctors in the Department of Health" is her objection to the view – expressed here by Katie's father (a "powerfully-built Scandinavian") – that "everyone had a right to propagate their kind, no matter how debased or marred the offspring might be" (178–9). McClung had made a similar argument regarding what she saw as a necessary restriction upon individual reproductive rights in *In Times Like These*: "A young man and a young woman say: 'I believe we'll get married!' and forthwith they do. The state sanctions it, and the church blesses it. They may be consumptive, epileptic, shiftless, immoral, or with a tendency to insanity. No matter. They may go on and reproduce their kind. They are perfectly free to bring children into the world, who are a burden and a menace to society. Society has to bear it – that is all!" (1915, 138–9)

Katie, in the 1945 vignette, is shown to have no right to "propagate [her] kind" not only because it would be what McClung described in 1915 as "an appalling crime against the innocent and the helpless" (141) but because her children would be "a burden and a menace to society." McClung records that a meeting was arranged with a doctor in the Department of Health (1945, 178), culminating in the father's signing the form for sterilization. "I saw Katie and her mother a year later," McClung concludes. "The mother looked younger and happier. Katie was well and neatly dressed. Her mother told me that she was taking full charge of the chickens now, and in the evenings was doing Norwegian knitting which had a ready sale in the neighborhood. The home was happy again" (180). McClung's story is a first-person account of eugenical intervention, and of the kind of work that can be done when a system of legislated sterilization is in place, as it was in Alberta until 1972. She demonstrates an obvious support for the system, and a certain pride in being able to intervene.

Fiamengo has rightly cautioned against "interpreting *The Stream Runs Fast* as a factual life record," given that "no solid evidence exists that [McClung] ever spoke on the matter [of eugenics] in the Legislature" (1999–2000, 78).[22] While it is important not to focus obsessively upon what is easily read as a damning articulation of racism, it is also important to take seriously this section of the autobiography, in which, after all, she is constructing a story of herself and her nation-building work. McClung's account of Katie is significant not only because of its explicitly stated support for Hoadley's bill but because of its narrative positioning of McClung as the figure behind the return of social and domestic order ("The home was happy again"). It is in effect less an explicit account of her work for the Sexual Sterilization Bill than a parable of what Saleeby called Eugenic Feminism. It shows the woman as mother of the race at work and shows the kind of work she is to do.

McClung's precise involvement in the history of eugenics in Canada is hard to locate because its traces are in widely scattered archives and in clippings.[23] Moreover, as the story of Katie reminds us, it is in her writing; and it is not only in the autobiography and in the suffrage manifesto *In Times Like These* but in her fiction. McClung made no secret of the fact that she saw her fiction to be fundamentally didactic; in fact, she believed *all* fiction should be concerned first with the instruction of its readers. In the same volume of her autobiography, she articulated her position on fiction in an anecdote that is regularly cited in the analysis of her literature "as pulpit," as Warne has put it. "I remember once in a discussion at a Canadian Authors' Convention," McClung wrote, "when I had been asked to speak on 'The Writers' Creed' I took the position that no one should put pen to paper unless he or she had something to say that would amuse, entertain, instruct, inform, comfort, or guide the reader. I was assailed with particular vehemence by one of my fellow members who is a writer of novels – she cried out in disgust: 'Who wants to write books for Sunday Schools? I certainly do not'" (1945, 70).

McClung, however, *did* see the writing of books for Sunday Schools – or at least morally guiding books – as not only a worthy but a vital undertaking. She takes this position in her ensuing vindication of "Sunday School libraries" as a crucial apparatus in the forging of the nation for white settlers in the early days of western expansion. When she describes her own early reading of "*Ivanhoe, The Talisman, Swiss Family Robinson, Children of the New Forest*, and *A Life of Livingstone*" (70), she implicitly conveys the notion that these libraries ensured the circulation of children's classics of English literature in the imagined new world, and thus facilitated in a vital way the culture of Anglo-Saxon imperialism. Children in western Canada would be inculcated, as she indicates she had been, into a tradition of "Saxondom" first through the reading of the same literature that Anglo-Saxon children everywhere were reading. McClung is righteous here less on theological grounds – the spread of Christianity through the distribution of Sunday school books – than on imperial ones. Her Canadian Authors' Association interlocutor is wrong, we are to see, because she has not recognized the investment of these same libraries in the civilizing mission and the spread of "the race."

In 1916 in an article in the *Canadian Magazine*, Norman P. Lambert described McClung as "a modern Joan of Arc" for a new nation:

Five hundred years ago, the Maid of Orleans, in response to a vision, donned the warrior's coat of armour, took up the sword and led the forces of her country against the hosts of the enemy in the cause of freedom. Armed with a facile pen and an eloquent tongue, instead of a sword and a battle-axe, Mrs. Nellie McClung to-day in Canada is leading forces of rapidly-increasing strength against the traditional foes and obstacles of certain social reforms. She, too, is being led by a vision: one which has grown in magnitude as her work has extended and increased in influence. It is the vision of a young nation which will give equal economic and political opportunity not only to all men, but also to all women. And associated in such a state is the picture of a new and enlarged democracy, purged of the evils of the liquor traffic and the impoverishing effect of a growing industrialism. (265)

Lambert's representation of McClung not only marks the early establishment of her work as a national undertaking with the general social good as its goal but it foregrounds her writing and speaking as the tools (or weapons) of her social reform. In fact, as an analysis of her eugenical ideas must show, her political work actually took place in large part in her fiction, which disseminated her "vision" and the principles upon which all of her work and her feminist activism must be seen to rest.

Lucy Bland has made the point that critics and historians have paid little attention to "fiction writing as itself a feminist activity. Yet with the rise of the 'new woman' novel [in the 1890s], many women began to write literature that was explicitly didactic and feminist" (1987, 143). Many "New Woman" novels, Bland intimates, should be regarded as tools in the struggle for women's rights, and works that undertook to expose the signs of "race" degeneration and to show how women *were* the way out: "Not only were the female 'new woman' writers generally feminists (and many were involved in various women's rights campaigns), but they openly wrote as such and believed [as Mary Haweis put it] their 'first duty as women writers [was] to help the cause of other women ... In women's hands – in women writers' hands – [lay] the regeneration of the world'" (143).[24] McClung's novels, as her explicit representation of her heroine Pearlie Watson as a "New Woman" indicates, are best understood within the category Bland delineates here, and they thus need to be read in terms of the "feminist activity" of what Haweis, cited above by Bland, refers to as the "regeneration of the world." For McClung the writing of didactic fiction was a crucial part of what she called "the social responsibility of woman" and one branch of the feminist's maternal and eugenic work in the context of empire.

All of McClung's longer fiction – the three Watson novels of 1908, 1910, and 1921 and *Painted Fires* of 1925 – is concerned first with the idea of woman as mother of the race, delineating her through the models of Pearlie Watson and, in the 1925 novel, Helmi Milander. McClung narrativizes the model mother's work as she brings other women to "think" and thus influences the condition of the community as a national and imperial locus for race-based expansionist growth. Indeed, there is very little of McClung's fiction that is *not* concerned with the representation of the mothers of the race who would save "Saxondom" from degeneration by leading the way to renewal. It is possible to see McClung's insistent representation of this figure in terms of the same apparatuses or, at least, discursive sites as the ones she promotes in *In Times Likes These*: feminism, mothercraft, and eugenics. McClung's feminism is generally informed by eugenical principles of "enlightened motherhood." The specifics of her eugenical work in Canada are to be found in her fictional representations of the West, and in her romantic narratives of women's work in the imperial mission on the frontier.

PART TWO

Reading Maternalism in McClung's Fiction
The Culture of Imperial Motherhood

Words are seeds, strong, fertile, fast growing seeds. When once they leave your pen or lips, who knows what the crop will be.

McClung, "The Writer's Creed"

4

"Finger-Posts on the Way to Right Living"
Mothering the Prairies

"– I blame the whole thing on these darned women!... Look! They've
got a society now at the Crossing, another at the Waterhole, another at
Spirit River. They get speakers from Edmonton, and travellin' libraries.
Then comes the nurses! livin' alone too, and that's no way for young
women to live! They tell the women what they should have, and
shouldn't have. Take my woman. She's lost four kids already ... always
was resigned – always said it was the Lord's will ... but now you
should hear her ... She used hard words ... bitter words ... harsh
words, the last time it was mentioned, said it was my fault for not
bringin' the doctor – and all that!"

McClung, *When Christmas Crossed "The Peace"*

Within the framework of expansionism and anxiety that the
"empty" imperial spaces could not be filled (Davin, 10), the newly
opened western Canadian provinces were imagined to be the British
empire's final frontier – or, as Ernest Thompson Seton put it in the
early century pro-British immigrationist magazine *Canada West*,
"the white man's last opportunity" (April 1908, 525–32). This territory was also represented propagandistically as the last *best* West:
it was the biggest, purest, richest colonial space ever. It was, as
Doug Owram has shown in *The Promise of Eden* (1980), touted
as a land of incredible resources, easily tapped, simple to farm. It
had been emptied of the "Indian" threat, and was ready to be taken
up by Anglo-Saxons who wished to avail themselves of the generous
offers made by Canadian governments anxious to fill the West with
white and especially British people. It was, many immigrationist

pamphlets argued, healthy and invigorating. Pulmonary diseases would be cured in the West; weakness would be eradicated. Canada, and especially Canada West, would serve the British empire as a location for the generation of a new and stronger community of Anglo-Saxons, a new world peopled by a sturdy branch of old-world peoples, into which revitalized stock would be assimilated all those who could vanish into the racial category of whiteness, and from which would be excluded all those seen to be unassimilable and, in a range of ways, "unfit."

British women had been wooed to the frontiers at least since the middle of the nineteenth century, when apparatuses such as the Female Middle Class Emigration Society began to take on the work of transporting middle-class women to the bachelors of the colonies.[1] White women were essential for populating the territories and making them Anglo-Saxon. Their perceived value in these settings is evident in the direct propagandist appeal to women to colonize the "new" imperial territories. It is also evident in the intense concern with protecting white women from sexual contact with native and non-white men in colonial settings.[2] To this end a number of official measures were undertaken: for example, the so-called "White Woman's Protection Ordinance" of Papua New Guinea, and the "White Woman's Labour Law" in Canada, restricting white women from working in Chinese-owned businesses in Canada.[3] Such legislation is comprehensible in relation to what Sarah Carter has shown to be an anxiety about women, reproduction, and race that was pervasive throughout the empire but arguably more intense in colonial and frontier settings.

The work of "psychic" motherhood, moreover, was constructed as even more vital to the maintenance of empire than comparable maternal work in the imperial centre. In the context of contact with native peoples and, in the settler colonies especially, with non-Anglo-Saxon immigrants, the development of "an enlightened culture of motherhood" was concomitantly urgent. White women in the colonies, as Antoinette Burton's important study of British feminists in India has demonstrated, were called to take up the civilizing mission and to exert their maternalism upon "lower" categories of people, and especially upon other women.[4] Their supposedly higher evolutionary status visibly marked in the perceived distinctions between themselves and women of colour (more oppressed, less educated, less evolved as a race), white women in the colonies could – and did

– make a compelling case for their necessary political empowerment as agents of empire and of eugenics. Their front-line work was not only to generate the new and better offspring who would carry the imperial work ever forward but to preserve the race and its morals in the colonial wildernesses. They were to block miscegenation, to lift up the lower "races," if not to equality at least to the status of well-behaved and grateful children, and most importantly, they were to mark and maintain the boundaries of whiteness.

Ann Laura Stoler has drawn attention to the way that in colonial settings "eugenic influence manifested itself ... in a translation of the political *principles* and the social values that eugenics implied": "Applied to European colonials, eugenic statements pronounced what kind of people should represent Dutch or French rule, how they should bring up their children, and with whom they should socialize. Those concerned with issues of racial survival and racial purity invoked moral arguments about the national duty of French, Dutch, British, and Belgian colonial women to stay home" (1997, 356–7).

Feminism, as McClung's work shows, responded to this imperative in the settler colonies with an affirmation of the point that maternal feminism was making throughout the empire: that it was not only at "home" that their work was necessary but throughout the social and political spheres where men had been dominant and, feminists held, too often destructive. According to colonial feminists, it was women – naturally maternal, the caregivers, the family's centre – who were best suited to make the kinds of "eugenic statements" Stoler indicates, *outside* of the home and in the context of the nation.

In a short story included in *Be Good to Yourself* (1930), McClung would make explicit her sense of the essential features of the figure of the mother-woman who put her maternal instinct to work for the improvement of "the race" in the West. The title "They Are Not All Married" highlights McClung's position that spiritual or "psychic" mothering was the best work for all women, and that women with children as well as without needed to recognize that female "duty" did not stop – or even begin – with reproduction. Indeed, in this story the unmarried heroine, Hilda Collins, is shown in favourable contrast to her married sisters, who have not seen that their work, if it is to be *racially* effective, also lies outside of their own homes. Hilda tends her sisters' children, teaches, effects more change through her active good work for the race than her sisters have done, and is in consequence happy and fulfilled: "When she began to teach, she found a fierce joy in bringing beauty where none had been before, for her first school was in one of the most desolate parts of the prairie misleadingly called Ferndell ... At the end of the second year, Ferndell school had a red roof, gleaming white walls, frilled curtains, a flagged walk, a hedge of caragana, small but hopeful, and flaming flower beds. She had a dramatic club among the young people; a reading circle for the women, and her school activities were featured in one issue of the *Teachers' Magazine*" (1930, 161–2).

By the middle of the story Hilda has been, like her world, "transformed" by "happiness," and made "almost pretty" by her satisfaction in "her work." By contrast, her "prettiest [married] sister" is shown to be one of the many idle and selfish women – the "Gentle Ladies" or, in Gilman's term, the "parasites" – of McClung's fictional repertoire, unhappy because she does not make herself useful. When this sister tells the narrator that Hilda "is going to England ... to lecture about Canada with all her expenses paid and a good salary," she also complains that Hilda is leaving *her* alone by going": "She knows I am not very strong, and I will miss her so. She doesn't seem to care. Women without children get so selfish!" "Selfish!" gasps the narrator. "Hilda Collins is one of the mothers of the race" (163).

Hilda's maternal function is emphasized when she describes her own feelings at the end of the story: "I have had such joy in my work. And the work is absorbing. I wish you could see some of the children in those families of mine!" (164). Hilda clearly has improved these "children" of "hers," as she has improved the world in which they are living, thus fulfilling the "two duties" of every woman that McClung delineated in her suffrage writing. Her sister, conversely, while a biological mother, has failed to accomplish the same kind of work. "I looked after [Hilda] in admiration as she went quickly down the street," the narrator concludes, "and I was more than ever convinced that the Lord knows what He is doing when He leaves some of the best women in the world unattached" (164). As McClung indicates here, there is crucial "mothering" work to be done by all women. This work is based upon an essentializing notion of maternal instinct that can be activated (at least, according to McClung and early twentieth-century psychoanalysis) in "normal" women, regardless of whether or not they are married or, less euphemistically, have children.[5]

The story "They Are Not All Married" foregrounds McClung's interest in circulating ideas of women's work for the advancement of "the race." It also demonstrates her primary strategy for a didactic eugenically feminist fiction: the invocation of a model who works within the narrative to instruct the reader. Hilda, after all, is a teacher. She is not only teaching "her children" in the story; she is also teaching readers of the story how to be like *her*. McClung, like other women writers working within the framework of eugenic feminism and maternalist ideology (L.M. Montgomery is a case in point), would make great use of the strategy of instructing her readers through a metonymic teacher identified explicitly or implicitly as a mother of the race. McClung utilizes this technique in her best-known fiction, the "Watson" trilogy: *Sowing Seeds in Danny* (1908), *The Second Chance* (1910), and *Purple Springs* (1921). In all these novels, model mother-women (not just the heroine Pearlie but a veritable army) are able, through teaching, to bring small communities and, by implication, the whole of the frontier West, the nation, and the empire to a new and higher level of civilization.

McClung published two novellas, *The Black Creek Stopping-House* in 1912 and *When Christmas Crossed "The Peace"* in 1923. Both are stories of "women's work" in the West, and both foreground the importance of women in the expansionist movement. Women's work, McClung implies, would build the West and preserve it as the last frontier of empire. *The Black Creek Stopping-House* is dedicated to the "godly Pioneer Women, who kept alive the conscience of the neighbourhood, and preserved for us the best traditions of the race" (3).[6] The book itself, in narrating these traditions, is also implicitly doing the work of preservation; its writer, moreover, is to be recognized as one of the "godly Pioneer Women."

At the centre of *The Black Creek Stopping-House* is the character of Maggie Corbett, who also features prominently in the later novel *Painted Fires* as one of the few who help the heroine Helmi Milander when she is alone and virtually penniless in the city. Maggie, when she first appears in the 1912 novella as Maggie Murphy, is a soldier of the Salvation Army in Winnipeg, selling the Salvation Army publication "War Crys" at the door (10). In this role she attracts the attention of a gambler, John Corbett, who is turned away from the "dark" path he has been following not by her entreaties but by her example: "Having watched Maggie Murphy wait on table in the daytime and sell *War Crys* at night for a week or more, Mr. Corbett decided he liked her methods" (12). He promises "to leave the cards alone" if she will marry him (12), and she does.

Maggie's service in the Salvation Army ends, but her function as a soldier of regeneration does not. Her "good works" are in fact the focus of the novella, and when she plucks a few more "brands ... from the burning" (12–13), it is clear that she is able to rescue these potentially lost souls not only because of her own maternal instinct but because she has learned to think about what to do. She thus epitomizes the kind of "trained motherly" women McClung valorizes in *In Times Like These* (1915, 133), and, although her children do not appear until *Painted Fires* (in this story she is not, as she puts it, "a mother after the flesh" [60]), her natural "mother-love" is much in evidence in her work. As she writes to Mr Robert Grant of the Imperial Lumber Company when she wants to reunite him with his daughter, "I like to take a hand any place I see I can do any good" (1912, 56).

Maggie is described as the "guardian of the morals of the neighbourhood" (20), and her "home mission" work in the expansionist West is given the same weight and effect as the "city mission" work that saved John Corbett for "the Lord [to] use ... to His honor and glory" (13). Her "Stopping-House" is thus allegorized as a meeting-place with a similar value to that of the Victoria Hall where the Salvation Army of the first chapter holds its meetings: it "gave not only food and shelter to the men who teamed the wheat to market, it gave them good fellowship and companionship" (16) – and more. Through Maggie Corbett, the Stopping-House gives the men directions for "right living": "Actions and events which seemed quite harmless, and even heroic, when discussed along the trail, often changed their complexion entirely when Mrs. Maggie Corbett let in the clear light of conscience on them, for even on the very edge of civilization there are still to be found finger-posts on the way to right living. Mrs. Maggie Corbett was a finger-post" (16). Her work, it is suggested, is desperately needed to save and redirect the young men who arrive under the "delusion that is so prevalent ... that Canada is a good, kind wilderness where iced tea is the strongest drink known, and where no more exciting game than draughts is ever played" (1912, 25).

The allegorical value of Maggie as a guardian of morals and of her Stopping-House as a missionary outpost "on the very edge of civilization" is emphasized in the representation of the creek "on

whose wooded bank the Stopping-House stands" (17). McClung is
not so much countering the immigrationist myth of Canada and
especially the "last best West" as inherently pure and, consequently,
purifying for its settlers as she is suggesting that mostly male settlement is necessarily attended by a lapse in the morals of the community. McClung makes the point with the image of the creek that
the "dangers" that lurk in the city are also to be found "on the
very edge of civilization": Black Creek "is a deep black stream ...
Here and there throughout its length are little shallow stretches
which show a golden braid down the centre like any peaceful
meadow brook where children may with safety float their little
boats, but Black Creek, with its precipitous holes, is no safe companion for any living creature that has not webbed toes or a guardian angel" (17). Maggie is such a guardian, and when she saves the
impetuous Mrs Brydon from abandoning her marriage, she also
saves the hope in and of the West as what McClung would always
call "the land of the second chance."[7]

Maggie's missionary work at the Stopping-House is undertaken
in such a way as to reveal her training under the auspices of the
Salvation Army. When she first attempts to divert Rance Belmont,
the atheist and epicurean "divil" who wants to tempt the unhappy
Mrs Brydon to leave her husband, she invokes the "One ... who
comes to help when all other help fails" (59–60). "There is a God,"
she tells Rance, "slowly and reverently, for she was Maggie Murphy
now, back to the Army days when God walked with her day by
day, 'and He can hear a mother's prayer, and through I was never
a mother after the flesh, I am a mother now to that poor girl in the
place of the one that's gone, and I'm askin' Him to save her, and
I've got me answer. He will do it.' There was a gleam in her eyes
and a white glow in her face that made Rance Belmont for one
brief moment tremble" (60).

Maggie is thus aglow with an unearthly and obviously divine
light. She appears "for one brief moment" as a madonna, albeit an
Anglo-Saxon and Protestant one, a motherly saviour of the last best
imperial nation. She reveals to Rance the error of his ways; and
while he is not "saved," the more worthy Brydons and their marriage are rescued, given, like the Watsons through the ministrations
of Pearl in the Watson trilogy, their "second chance."

Maggie is configured, like Hilda Collins, as a mother of the race,
her desire to save both Rance and Mrs Brydon from corruption a

natural outpouring of maternal instinct, biological but not necessarily performed in reproduction. Her work is shown to be solidly grounded in an ethics of cleanliness and godliness. It is Maggie's instinct to clean and to care for her society, her putatively maternal desires that compel her to take up the work of filtering malevolent and racially counterproductive elements through her Stopping-House. The same kind of purifying work is undertaken by Nurse Downey in *When Christmas Crossed "The Peace."* Ostensibly a temperance tale, this novella is the story of an early public health nurse in the Peace District of north-western Alberta who drives alcohol out of the settlement and sets it and the frontier it represents on the path to health and happiness. In its narrative trajectory and its "moral," this novella is similar to stories such as E. Pauline Johnson's "Mother o' the Men," which shows a self-sacrificing and unquestionably motherly woman who keeps her "boys" on the north-western frontier from drinking and thus ruining themselves and, implicitly, the future of the nation (*The Moccasin Maker*, 180–94).

McClung's novels and stories have been treated for many years less as literary works than as "historical documents." Her skills as a writer have been regularly downplayed or denigrated, and her fiction discussed in terms of what it conveys about its own context – politically in its account of circumstances and events, ideologically in its representation of gender, suffragism, the West, settlement, immigration, and assimilation. McClung's fiction has been cited in studies of nativism (Howard Palmer), social reform (Mariana Valverde), feminism (Catherine Cleverdon and Carol Lee Bacchi), and eugenics (Angus McLaren); and, like much New Woman and feminist fiction from the 1880s to the 1930s, its value has tended to inhere in what it "tells" us about its period and about the politics of its author. But McClung's writing *is* fiction: it is engaged with a set of literary conventions, and functions within a particular tradition of settler narrative. It is evident, as Warne has shown, that McClung saw fiction as the most important tool for social reform; it is also clear that she saw herself as a political *artist*, producing social change through her work.

If McClung's feminism is best understood as an imperial politics embedded in ideas of race preservation and eugenics that could only be effectively implemented through the control of reproduction by and for women, what Marilyn Davis has called her "fiction of a feminist" is best understood in the same terms. That is, McClung's writing too is imperialist: her narratives are constructed as imperial adventures, stories of settlement, romances of colonization, but they are, as Davis has also suggested, "subversive." For Davis their subversiveness lies in their countering of patriarchy configured as a political system opposing equal rights for women in Canada. What they might be seen to be subverting as well, however, are the conventions of contemporary imperial genres, thus making a eugenic feminist fiction. While representing the same "problems" – of social hygiene, alcoholism, family violence, immigration, "Indians," masculinity and lawlessness in the West, diseases such as tuberculosis – that figure in so much fiction of the period, they do so with a maternal feminist New Woman at the centre.

In a 1919 article in the *Canadian Bookman*, English-Canadian critic E.J. Hathaway outlined his view of "How Canadian Novelists Are Using Canadian Oppportunities." It was, he suggested,

in the vast north and west beyond the sky line, where the strange ways go down, that the most characteristic of Canadian fiction is to be found. Here are adventure and hardship, romance and struggle. Here are hardy and adventurous Hudson's Bay factors and voyageurs; picturesque "breeds" and red-skinned braves, rugged trappers and traders who for generations threaded the trails and followed the water courses; red-coated mounted police who carried law and order into the frontier places and made settlement possible; hardy and venturesome settlers who pioneered the way into the prairies and laid the foundations for the cities and towns that were to be. (21)

Hathaway's gendering of the fictional "opportunities" of the West is obvious, and, while he does go on to mention McClung's first two novels in his account of stories of prairie life, it is also obvious that her fiction does not quite fit into the romantic and imperial framework he outlines here. *When Christmas Crossed "The Peace"* shows McClung significantly subverting the conventional settler narrative, such as Ralph Connor produced, of purity in the West maintained through the intervention of the male lawgiver. McClung's Nurse Downey is already doing crucial work: her assaults on the community's hygiene, at personal and collective, bodily and moral levels are represented as the vital work of protecting the frontier for settlement and reproduction. She also performs (literally) the work that would have been done by her male counterpart, a sergeant of the Alberta

Provincial Police. When he falls and hurts his leg, she puts on his uniform and gets his man. She rides off into the night, corners the villain Bill on his way to buy liquor for all the local men, handcuffs him, takes his roll of money, and then compels him to spend it on a Christmas treat for the community. Her gender-crossing is important. Nurse Downey can do the work of both men and women, professionally and competently, but she can also do the work of her male counterpart *better* because she knows how to take charge of the problem and make it into something beneficial, curative, and restorative.

As this novel and so many others suggest, the West provided a particular Canadian opportunity for first-wave feminism. The need for white women on the frontier had been widely advertised since the 1870s. A good deal of propaganda was aimed at attracting white women to the prairies as a work of imperial "duty"; but it was also implicitly presented as a location where women could leave behind "old world" gender restrictions and find a new freedom. Such, at any rate, is how McClung and other women writers of the period configured the West. This perceived freedom was a sign of the potential for imperial or "racial" advancement in the West (insofar as a "civilization" was perceived to be as "advanced" as its women). It was also an indication that there *were* opportunities for women in the West, doing the kind of work McClung outlined in *In Times Like These*. This work was not necessarily reproductive but professional, and, if broadly "maternal," nonetheless a way to independence and "racial" service.

McClung, the most influential and widely read feminist of the first wave in English Canada, was also arguably the most direct in her didacticism. She configured maternal agents of empire within romantic and imperial narratives that represented in didactic terms the growth and education – and, importantly, their effects on other women – of the mother of the race.[8] The emergence of what should be understood as a maternalist, eugenist genre in English Canada was a crucial element in producing the shift in the imperial ideology of motherhood around the time of the Boer War. According to fiction such as McClung's about mother-women on the frontiers, the "adventure" of empire could be – or, according to feminists, *had* to be – understood as a gynocentric political process that revolved around a romanticized narrative of reproduction but was played out in the work of women to "cure," as Maggie Corbett and Nurse Downey both do, the new imperial nation of its "racial poisons."

5

Pearlie Watson and Eugenic Instruction in the Watson Trilogy
How to Be a Maternal Messiah of the New World

Scatter diligently in susceptible minds
· The germs of the good and beautiful;
They will develop there to trees,
Bud, bloom and bear
The golden fruit
Of paradise.
Arthur W. Beall, *The Living Temple:*
A Manual on Eugenics for Parents and Teachers, 1933

McClung's first novel, *Sowing Seeds in Danny*, published in 1908, was enormously popular.[9] By 1924, J.D. Logan and Donald French maintained that it was one of five works of fiction published that year heralding "the second Renaissance" of English-Canadian literature (1924, 298–9).[10] By 1939 the 1911 William Briggs edition had gone into seventeen printings. It was in print as late as 1972.

Sowing Seeds in Danny, as the title intimates, is about what eugenists referred to as "race culture." McClung was tenacious in retaining her title for the novel, which her publisher, Thomas Allen, saw as unwieldy and awkward. Such a title was necessary, however, if the book was to be understood in terms of what McClung saw as the national project of "growing a race" and what she would maintain was the importance of situating that work in the hands of the appropriate women (*Maclean's*, July 1916, 38). If, as Bland has pointed out, the "central positive eugenic strategy" "was educational" (1995, 232), in one very important sense McClung's first novel functions in a way that is not unlike more overtly educational eugenical manuals such as the one cited in this chapter's epigraph. Ontario school inspector Arthur W. Bealls begins his 1933 book with the metaphor of seeds and racial growth. The process he describes is also comprehensible as what McClung calls "sowing seeds in Danny," a work she puts squarely in the hands of women. But it is a process about which, she indicates, many women might need a word of advice from good motherly women.

McClung's Pearlie Watson is the epitome of the feminist figure of the mother of the race in early twentieth-century English Canadian literature. Only L.M. Montgomery's exactly contemporary heroine, Anne Shirley, vies with Pearl as a national literary model of superior maternalist qualities.[11] Pearl, when she first appears in *Sowing Seeds in Danny*, is a twelve-year-old girl who is already "second mother of all the little Watsons" (294), caring for her eight younger siblings "six days in the week" (11) while their mother works in the home of a middle-class woman. Uncomplaining, bright, imaginative, hard-working, given to cheery applications of exemplary personal and domestic hygiene, Pearl is first seen washing her youngest brother, the eponymous Danny (11). It is clear from the beginning that she is positioned as "naturally a guardian of the race," and someone to whom the community might – and should, if it wants to survive and prosper – look for advice. Her impulse to clean is presented as explicitly social: in the chapter "The Live Wire" (an early short story by McClung),[12] Pearlie is shown washing dishes, and her imaginative narrative of how she views herself while she washes simultaneously indicates her mature acceptance of the necessity of such work and her sense that cleaning always has broader implications. Women's housework epitomizes, that is, their work for the larger community. "When I sweep the floor," she says, "I pertend I'm the army of the Lord that comes to clear the way from dust and sin, let the King of Glory in. Under the stove the hordes of sin are awful thick, they love darkness rather than light, because their deeds are evil! But I say the 'sword of the Lord and of Gideon!' and let them have it!" (106).

Despite the seemingly light and mocking treatment of Christian social reform, the suggestion McClung makes here is serious. Pearlie's vision of her work is evocative of McClung's argument in *In Times Like These*, that "if women ever get into politics there will be a cleaning-out of pigeon-holes and forgotten corners, on which the dust of years has fallen, and the sound of the political carpet-beater will be heard in the land" (1915, 66). Thus positioned as an incipient mother of the race, Pearl's advice and its effects are the focus of the novel. Ostensibly following the lines of the fortunes of the "rising" Watson family as they attempt to make their way and boost the empire by farming a section in Manitoba, the narrative is constructed as a more or less episodic sequence of conversions and benevolent works performed by Pearl.

The novel begins with Pearl's conversion of Mrs J. Burton Francis, described in the opening list of the "People of the Story" as "a dreamy woman, who has beautiful theories" (1908, ix). These, it is quickly made evident, have to do with ideas of motherhood. Pearl sets in motion a series of events that will lead to the awakening of "mother-love" in Mrs Francis. If the short story "They Are Not All Married" shows an exemplary "mother of the race" in Hilda Collins, *Sowing Seeds in Danny* charts the process of producing such a woman from a well-intentioned but misguided candidate.

Like Hilda, Mrs Francis is childless. Like Hilda, she embraces the creed of first-wave feminist "psychic" motherhood. Although she thus significantly represents the feminist context from which McClung herself is working, Mrs Francis also represents the woman of the period whom McClung most deplored, the Gentle Lady or the "clubwoman," someone who belonged to many useful organizations but did not effect much change or much good.[13] Her heart, we are told, "was kind, when you could get to it; but it was so deeply crusted over with theories ... that not very many people knew that she had one" (1908, 38). Mrs Francis, as we soon see, does not turn her "lofty ideals" into useful actions. She is guilty, as Pearlie would put it, of "faith without works" (1910, 293); she is guilty, like the woman in L.M. Montgomery's short story "Penelope Struts Her Theories," of not practising the *real* work of mothering.[14]

When we first meet Mrs Francis, she has been reading up on "Purposeful Motherhood" in a book by a Dr Ernestus Parker.[15] Inspired, she suggests that Pearl's mother, who does her washing, should read the book "and explain it to [her husband], it would be so helpful to [them] both, and so inspiring. It deals so ably with the problems of child-training" (1908, 6–7). The theoretical approach to mothering taken by both Dr Parker and his disciple is shown, like Penelope's theories for the heroine in Montgomery's story, to have little relevance to the real "perplexities" of mother-hood. Mrs Watson is far more concerned with such problems as "how to make trousers for four boys out of the one old pair the minister's wife had given her; how to make the memory of the rice-pudding they had on Sunday last all the week; how to work all day and sew at night and still be brave and patient; how to make little Danny and Bugsey forget they were cold and hungry. Yes, Mrs. Watson had her problems; but they were not the kind that Dr. Ernestus Parker had dealt with in his book on 'Motherhood'" (7).

Mrs Francis does not see the discrepancy between her ideals and their implementation in the Watson household, any more than she has perceived the irony in her advising Mrs Watson to "be very careful of your health, and not overdo your strength" (4) as she sends her toiling up and down the stairs so she may tell her about the "Beauty of Motherhood" (8). It is Mrs Watson herself who draws attention to the disjunction between Mrs Francis's idealism and its worth to the potential improvement of either "the race" or "the world." "D'ye think," she asks her children, "a foine lady like her would be bothered with the likes of us? She is r'adin' her book, and writin' letthers, and thinkin' great thoughts, all the time. When she was speakin' to me today she looked at me so wonderin' and faraway I could see that she thought I wasn't there at all at all, and me farninst [in front of] her all the time" (17). It is what is before her that Mrs Francis must be brought to see if she is to perform her duties as a mother of the race.

The didactic implications of *Sowing Seeds in Danny* are suggested in the opening chapter's positioning of Mrs Francis as the text's metonymic reader and thus the object of the novel's instruction. This chapter bears, after all, the same title as the novel itself, and should be seen to be establishing the basis for its teaching. However, the metonymic "sermon" in this opening chapter is not, signifi-cantly, Mrs Francis's own "uplifting talk on motherhood" (11). Nor is it to be found in either the ill-fated "little red book" in which she records her dubious accomplishments for a "report for her department at the next Annual Convention of the Society for Prop-agation of Lofty Ideals" (8). (For example, she writes after her "talk" with Mrs Watson, "Dec. 7, 1903. Talked with one woman today *re* Beauty of Motherhood. Recommended Dr. Parker's book. Believe good done" [8].) Nor is the sermon contained in the "great book by Dr. Ernestus Parker, on 'Motherhood'" (6). If Mrs Francis is the metonymic white middle-class woman reader whose lesson is also the reader's, Pearlie is the metonymic woman writer, for Mrs Francis's conversion is accomplished through twelve-year-old Pearlie's telling of the story of the "pink lady."[16] That is, Pearl's "story," like McClung's, is to be regarded as a practical tool for the work of bringing women to an understanding of their duty.

For McClung the social responsibility of women was not separable from the didactic work of the writer who was also a woman: her fiction had to take up the service of the race. Pearl shows her readers this service, in part through her own actions but also through her recording of them in her own "little red book," which she keeps as a record during her sojourn with the Motherwells (230). Pearl functions, thus, in effect, as the representative of the woman writer in whose hands "lies the regeneration of the world." Configured from the beginning as a child in whom the "maternal instinct was strong" (59), Pearl is shown in this first novel to be an incipient "mother-woman," instinctively compelled to perform maternalist work in the story and thus to perform the work that McClung saw as central to the writer's duty: to "amuse, entertain, instruct, inform, comfort, or guide the reader" (1945, 70).

Despite Mrs Watson's warning to the children that Mrs Francis would not "be bothered with the likes of us," Pearlie's story, which she, like McClung, is telling, *does* come true when she is made to tell it to Danny in front of Mrs Francis herself. Danny identifies her as the pink lady, and when Mrs Francis recognizes herself and her shortcomings and the Watsons' real needs as they are represented in Pearlie's story, she is perceptibly awakened:

> There was a strange flush on Mrs. Francis's face, and a strange feeling stirring her heart, as she hurriedly rose from her chair and clasped Danny in her arms.
>
> "Danny! Danny!" she cried, "you shall see the yellow birds, and the stairs, and the chocolates on the dresser, and the pink lady will come to-morrow with the big parcel."
>
> Danny's little arms tightened around her neck.
>
> "It's her," he shouted. "It's her." (1908, 29)

With this awakening, catalyzed by the story, Mrs Francis actually *becomes* the pink lady of the Watson children's ideal: her "strange flush" turns her pink, as it also marks the "strange feeling stirring her heart." That this process is a maternal epiphany is made emphatically clear: "When little Danny's arms were thrown around her neck, and he called her his dear sweet, pink lady, her pseudo-intellectuality broke down before a power which had lain dormant. She had always talked a great deal of the joys of motherhood ... But it was the touch of Danny's soft cheek and clinging arms that brought to her the rapture that is so sweet it hurts, and she realised that she had missed the sweetest thing in life" (38–9).[17]

This symbolic awakening of Mrs Francis's hitherto untapped maternal resources is further emphasized by the foregrounding of the image of the "Madonna on the wall" that "seemed to smile at her as she passed" (29). The picture of the Madonna also opens this chapter, a motif on the wall of Mrs Francis's "comfortable sitting room" that serves to iconize all women in terms of maternity (3). The "new warmth and tenderness" that the "glory of the short winter afternoon" brings to the face of the Madonna in the first lines is also brought to Mrs Francis when the "strange flush" lights her face as she finds the hidden well-spring of her maternalism. What is revealed in Mrs Francis is the "mother-love" (38) that has "lain dormant," and that, as McClung indicates when she suggests that "every normal woman desires children" (1915, 25), was to be seen as being natural. Once activated, this "tiny flame of real love" could "shed its beams among the debris of cold theories," and so Mrs Francis is converted into a beacon of light, a mother of the race, and, finally, another spoke in the wheel of progress.

Thus the Gentle Lady is converted to pink lady and joins the ranks of organized mother-love already forming around Pearl and a handful of other women in the town of Millford (notably Mary Barner, the doctor's daughter and leader of the wctu children's unit, the Band of Hope, and Camilla, housekeeper and moral guide for Mrs Francis). Little Danny, who instigates the recovery of her dormant maternalism, becomes a figure representative of the future of the race, and "sowing seeds" in him is now a process that must be undertaken by all women. Mrs Watson and Pearlie as well as Mrs Francis and Camilla all direct their energies towards Danny and his needs. Mrs Francis comes to see that this care is a process that requires both "mental food" and real nourishment. If she is to "speak to his young mind and endeavour to plant the seeds of virtue and honesty in that fertile soil" (1908, 19–20) as she indicates is her ambition, she is going to have to first speak to the fact that

"Danny is hungry" (27). This is a matter, as McClung would put it in *In Times Like These*, of looking after "the children who are already here" (1915, 140), of taking up the practical work of mothercraft rather than the "lofty theories" of motherhood that initially attract and mislead Mrs Francis.

At the end of the novel Mrs Francis does return to her theories and to Dr Parker's book on "Purposeful Motherhood" (1908, 61). She fishes into the waste-paper basket for her little red notebook, thrown away in a symbolic rejection of her "great thoughts" at the end of chapter 1, and refers to it again for advice. However, it is suggested that through the immediate effects of her practical benevolence for the Watsons, she has learned to "think" about the ideas of Dr Parker, or to see what is right in front of her. The book ends as it begins with Mrs Francis, but with her "motherly" facilitating of the union of the housekeeper, Camilla, and her sturdy suitor, Jim. Mrs Francis arranges for her husband to offer Jim a partnership, thus enabling the two to marry. "She held out a hand to each of them," we are told in the concluding lines. "'I do see – things – sometimes,' she said" (313). By the end of the novel, then, Mrs Francis is shown to have learned her early lesson well and to have been successfully trained in the kind of maternal social engineering of which Pearlie is a natural and instinctive practitioner.

Pearl, for her part, once she has ensured through her conversion of the pink lady that her young charges will be well looked after, moves in with the Motherwell family, to work off a ten-dollar debt still outstanding on the rail car in which the Watson family live on their section of land. Pearl teaches Mrs Motherwell how to do what she does *not* do well: Mrs Motherwell learns from Pearl, as Mrs Francis did, how to find and use her "maternal instinct." In her case, she learns to influence her husband, who is notoriously mean, and to help her son, who has turned to alcohol for release from the dessicated family life his parents have provided. Pearl awakens Mrs Motherwell's "instinct" by showing her the way that she, as a mother of the race, ought to direct her care and energy towards all the young people in her charge. Pearl has been brought to the farm to work off the debt because the Motherwell's English "girl," Polly, had been taken to the hospital in Winnipeg in what are clearly the last stages of consumption. When Pearl finds out that the poppies which are the only thing of beauty on the Motherwell farm were planted by the homesick Polly, she picks some and arranges for them to be brought to Polly in the hospital. They arrive only hours before the girl dies.

Mrs Motherwell reads the letter sent to her by a nurse in the hospital, thanking her for her kindness to the girl and telling her about Polly's joy at seeing the flowers. She begins, as McClung might put it, "to think": "That night she dreamed of Polly, confused, troubled dreams; now it was Polly's mother who was dead, then it was her own mother, dead thirty years ago" (232). Increasingly conscious of her shortcomings in her treatment of Polly while she was alive, when she "guiltily" finds the girl's letters from her mother, "something gather[s] in her throat" (237), and she realizes that she and her husband have erred in not tending to the children in their care – her own as well as other women's. "We didn't deserve the praise the [nurse] gave us," she sobs to her husband. "We didn't send the flowers, we have never done anything for anybody and we have plenty, plenty" (240). Her awakening to responsibility is followed by her husband's: when she weeps to him about their unkindness, "a mysterious Something, not of the earth ... struggle[s] with him" (240). Pearlie has been able to convince Mrs Motherwell of what a travelling book agent had not when he tried to sell her "a book entitled 'Woman's Influence in the Home'" (191). Mrs Motherwell, taught by Pearl, has learned to exert her influence as she ought and has made her husband a better man and her home a better place. The outspreading effects of their conversion are immediate: she and her husband perform their first good work, sending "a check for one hundred dollars, payable to Polly's mother" (241) to keep her from the poorhouse.

Although Pearl is too late to save English Polly, she does rescue a young English farmer in training, Arthur Wemyss, who represents renewed hope for the progress of Saxondom. Arthur nearly dies of appendicitis. Pearl's act of saving him, like Maggie's work in *The Black Creek Stopping-House*, has multiple and pervasive effects upon the community. Pearl's work is to stay by Arthur while Tom Motherwell, who was to have gone for the doctor, spends the night in a bar instead. Dr Barner, the local senior doctor and a heavy drinker, is not called at all. Pearl watches all night for the return of the younger Dr Clay, whom she has seen ride past on his way to see another patient. When he finally arrives, he has been shattered by what he thinks is his misdiagnosis of the other patient, who has died. He will not operate on Arthur. Pearl prays: "O God, dear God ... don't go back on us, dear God. Put the gimp into Doc again; he's not scared to do it, Lord, he's just lost his grip for a minute ... You can bank on Doc, Lord" (269–70). Dr Clay operates; Arthur lives. Dr Clay and Dr Barner, who has resented the younger practitioner, are reconciled. The older man, moreover, awakens to his own shortcomings caused by excessive drinking. His consciousness of this is inspired not only by Clay's successful operation on Arthur but by the discovery that Tom Motherwell had failed to fetch him because he was too drunk.

Pearl's saving of Arthur, an act with so many implications for the whole community, also thus "saves" Tom, who now will not have the Englishman's death on his conscience. Pearl is rewarded for her work with a cheque for £120 from Arthur's grateful parents; this money will enable her in future to turn over the childcare to her mother and go to school. The real reward, however, is the moral uplifting of the community of empire-builders that Pearl's actions have effected, and the implications all her work will have for the filling of this protected and purifying imperial space with children. Tom, recovered to sobriety and good works, with his renewed parents, is freed to marry Nellie Slater in the next novel. The narrative begun in the first instalment will find a number of romantic conclusions in marriages as happy – and, for the purposes of the "advancement" of "the race," as eugenic – as the unions of Jim and Camilla and the Reverend Hugh Grantley and WCTU Band of Hope leader Mary Barner at the end of *Sowing Seeds in Danny*.

Arthur's potential for the West is played out as the central drama in the next novel, *The Second Chance* (1910), which focuses on Pearl's manipulation of his romantic life in order to effect a desirable and eugenic marriage. In this sequel Arthur is brought by Pearl to recognize that his first choice for a wife, the fashionable and flighty English Thursa, is less in his real interests – and those of the community and the empire he represents – than the plainer but more maternal Canadian Martha, who can make good bread, sew, keep a house, and bear sturdy children. This novel's promoting of a eugenic marriage for Anglo-Saxon colonists is implicit in its renaming for sale in Britain in 1923 as *The Beauty of Martha*, a telling reconfiguring of the narrative. Martha *is* Arthur's "second chance," but the opportunity she presents is regenerative; in foregrounding this quality over the other "second chances" in both of these narratives – Dr Barner's at saving lives, the Motherwells' at empire-building, Mrs Francis's at "Purposeful Motherhood," Sandy Braden's at countering the dysgenic effects of drink, Libby Anne Cavers's at life after tuberculosis – the renaming also positions the novel, like all of McClung's novels, as a romance of reproduction, or, that is, a story of eugenical marriage with allegorical implications for the spread of "the race."

The opening chapter of McClung's first book embeds not only the story of *Sowing Seeds in Danny* but the entire three-part Watson narrative within a discourse of maternalism clearly to be understood as "feminism on the eugenic principle." Pearl's work of influencing Millford's unreclaimed mothers is to be seen to benefit not only her community but, we are to see, "the race" whose fortunes teeter in the balance in the West. This specifically eugenic maternalism underpins all of McClung's fiction, in its sustained narrative of imperial regeneration through women's moral and Christianizing work as well as through reproduction, and in its constitution of the woman writer as herself exerting maternal influence upon incipient national subjects through the circulation of directives pertaining to moral and social hygiene. In the Watson trilogy, this task is undertaken by Pearlie Watson, who represents the "fine type" of woman who needs no words of advice, and who, from prepubescence, dispenses them to those who are seen to need it.

The eugenic principles of McClung's romantic narratives are indicated in their playing out against a backdrop of dysgenic pressures: "the race" on the frontiers of the empire in Millford, Manitoba, is in serious danger of decline. "King Alcohol" has made headway in the community, "poisoning" even the town's senior doctor. It is up to Pearlie Watson to cure the community by eradicating racial poisons, something she can only do through the achievement of the vote. The concluding two novels of the trilogy make clear that this is the real end of the feminist work of organizing mother-love.

The mother of the race in these novels, the primary agent in reform and regeneration, puts an end to the problem of alcohol as both the "bed" of tuberculosis and a corrupting influence upon the community. She "wins through" the political impediments of anti-suffragism and "male statecraft" and leads her community and, by implication, her nation, to a new day in which the moral and physical diseases afflicting "the race" no longer adversely affect its future. In *Painted Fires*, McClung draws attention to "white slavery," a system of entrapping white women into prostitution, as, like alcohol consumption, an index and a cause of racial deterioration. It would not be possible to "grow a race" if the mothers of the race were not adequately protected.

In this novel, the ideal mother, Helmi Milander, wins through the sexual dangers thrown in her way and leads her community to a new level of racial and social purity. In her four novels, then, McClung took up the questions central to the eugenic feminist project: not only, that is, the political advancement of women but the work they would do for "the race" once they had the ability to do it. This work was both "positive" and "negative": it was concerned with breeding *in* good, solid racial characteristics such as Helmi and Pearl possess; it was also concerned with breeding *out* the problems – the "poisons," the diseases, the effects of dysgenic unions, the elements seen to be incompatible with the preservation and the promotion of Saxondom.

Teresa Mangum has outlined what she calls "the eugenic plot" in the later "new woman" novels of Sarah Grand.[18] "True" marriage, Mangum suggests, "had always been one object for Grand's characters, even though the novels focus on failed marriages. Marriage assumes an even more important task in the ... last novels [*Adnam's Orchard* and *The Winged Victory*]; marriage between genetically superior partners promises not only individual happiness but a future 'race' that will be too intelligent and sensible to permit oppression of any kind" (194–5). "True" marriage also promised the growth of a physically improved "race." McClung had made her position clear in *In Times Like These* on the hazards of leaving "marriage, homemaking, and the rearing of children ... entirely to chance" (1915, 141). These were precisely the areas in which feminists were to intervene, to counter the effects of "masculinity" on these "department[s] of life" (141). Her four novels and two novellas are all romantic narratives that end in happy unions; they do a particular kind of work as didactic narratives of eugenic feminism. They should also be seen in terms of what Mangum calls "the eugenic plot," bringing together the "fit" for the advancement of "the race," in this case, in its last best West.[19]

Eugenical feminist work as McClung defined it was a practical undertaking: women, empowered with the vote, would move swiftly to eradicate the racial poisons and racial diseases that were the causes and the symptoms of too much masculinity. Fiction was a tool in this work. It would perform the effective public expression of the problems and their solutions as they lay in the hands of women. English-Canadian women's fiction as McClung understood it was thus not only a matter of *writing* empire, narrating the heroine's adventures in social hygiene, but of *righting* empire. Fiction would produce palpable social change on an imperial and racial scale. It was not simply an articulation but an act of imperial social reform, and the basis for gendered agency within the context of empire.

PART THREE

Eugenic Plots
Feminist Work and the "Racial Poisons"

We were so sure that better home conditions, the extension of education and equality of opportunity would develop a happy race of people who would not be dependent on spurious pleasures.

"These things shall be, a nobler race
Than e'er the world has seen shall rise,
With flame of freedom in their hearts
And light of battle in their eyes."

We believed that with all our hearts as we went singing up the hill.

McClung, *The Stream Runs Fast*

6

"The Great White Plague" in the "Last Best West"

Tuberculosis, Temperance, and Woman Suffrage in *Purple Springs*

McClung's investment in a suffrage politics that saw the vote for women not as an indicator of gender-based "advancement" but as a "vestibule" leading to the higher evolution of the race is most evident in the way that her one explicitly suffrage-based novel, *Purple Springs* (1921), focuses less on the achievement of the vote than on what female enfranchisement would achieve. The third instalment in the story of Pearlie Watson, *Purple Springs* has usually been read as recounting the struggle for female enfranchisement in the West and as a fictionalized representation of McClung's own work in Manitoba in the years before 1916. But the book, written after the fact of provincial enfranchisement and a year after federal woman suffrage, should not be understood only as a nostalgic memorialization of the push for the vote. With the other novels of the trilogy, which *were* written in the suffrage years, it has work to do. J.D. Logan and Donald French condemned the novel as "politico propagandist" (1924, 303), but its "propaganda" could not in 1921 be directed at female enfranchisement. *Purple Springs* is rather about what women should be doing *with* the vote. According to McClung, they should be eradicating the "racial poisons" from the West.

Tuberculosis figures in the background of so much late nineteenth- and early twentieth-century literature in English that it is easy to overlook the extent to which its representation serves as an index of what was at the time a profound concern about the spread and the effects of this disease within the British Empire. Tuberculosis, or as it was called, consumption, or, more significantly, the "Great White Plague" or the "White Scourge," was one of a range of causes for widespread alarm about the strength of "the race." Along with alcohol, drugs, and venereal disease, it was considered to be a racial poison on the rise as the birth rate in the imperial centre appeared to be in decline. By the first decade of the century the White Plague was seen to indicate and be hastening the processes of imperial degeneration.[1] Anxiety about consumption made itself known in English Canada in the later years of the nineteenth century and the early years of the twentieth, and, as was the case in England, this anxiety would increasingly be inscribed in fiction and especially in imperial popular fiction.[2]

The novels of eastern Ontario writer Agnes Maule Machar (1837–1927), for instance, demonstrate concern with what was seen to be the disease's "relation to man and his civilization," as John Bessner Huber put it in the title of his 1906 manual on consumption. Machar's heroine in her 1870 novel, *Katie Johnstone's Cross*, bears the disease as a "cross" that inspires her to alert those about her to the need for the "home missions" work she is unable to perform. The work of empire, Katie implies, must be carried on. The immensely popular "Anne" books by L.M. Montgomery likewise signal the presence of the disease and its implications. The death of Anne's school chum Ruby Gillis in the third novel, *Anne of the Island* (1915), serves as a crucial interruption in the narrative and the point at which Anne's desires definitively shift from the pursuit of her own literary hopes to the maternal ideal. While works such as these show the same expansionist fears about the disease and its effects upon the race that underlie its literary representation in Britain throughout the nineteenth century, consumption by the early twentieth century was also significantly *re*-configured in some English-Canadian imperial fiction, notably in McClung's.

At least since the 1860s claims were made that Canada's northern climate could help restore an enervated race emigrating from abroad. As Carl Berger has pointed out, "Canada was to be a kind of rejuvenator of the imperial blood" (1966, 17), a place from which to generate a stronger, fitter breed of Anglo-Saxons.[3] So, at any rate, R.G. Haliburton had argued as early as 1869 in a lecture on "The Men of the North and Their Place in History." "The Northmen of the New World," Haliburton maintained, would revive "the old

stock" and emerge as "a hardy, a healthy, a virtuous, a daring, and
... a dominant race" (10). By the mid-1880s, these ideas – what poet
William Henry Taylor would characterize in 1913 as the "sanitary
virtues of the [Northern] sky" (cited in Berger 3) – were entrenched
in immigrationist propaganda of the West. For instance, in an 1886
pamphlet that provided its readers with accounts of *What Women
Say of the Canadian North-West,* a section on climate contains sixty-
seven comments virtually all affirming the health-giving qualities of
the air. Many of these women maintain that pulmonary complaints
such as tuberculosis improve after a short time in the West.[4] "It is
very healthy for consumptive people," observes Mrs T. Bowman of
Greenwood, Manitoba; indeed, she says, "It could not possibly be
more healthy" (15). Mrs S. Finn of Morris concurs: "Bracing atmo-
sphere is just the thing for young people with weak lungs, and this
is free from humidity" (16). And Mrs C.B. Slater of Wapella
concludes: "Excellently, exceedingly healthy" (18).[5]

It was not only immigrationist rhetoric, however, that took up
the notion of Canada and especially western Canada as a regenerative site for Saxondom. By the mid-1880s, imperial medical discourse had undertaken to "prove" the special purity of the North
West. Berger cites a series of papers published in 1884 by Montreal
physician William Hales Hingston under the title *The Climate of
Canada and Its Relation to Life and Health.* "Employing statistics
provided by the surgeons at British and American army stations,"
Berger notes of Hingston, "he ascertained that as one passed northward the salubrity of the climate increased, that the ratios of mortality from digestive, respiratory and nervous disorders decreased
in a northward progression." According to Hingston, "The dry air
and cold winter, moreover, [were] decided recuperators" of such
diseases as consumption (11). The tubercle bacillus had been isolated by Koch in 1882, but a cure had not yet been developed. Thus
Hingston's claims for the North held out hope against the spread
of the White Scourge.

By the 1920s the eugenical value of this putatively race-improving,
TB-curing part of the empire was clear. A few years after World
War I, Saleeby in a small monograph called *Sunlight and Health*
drew attention to "A Canadian Lesson" in "Light and Cold." Like
many of his contemporaries, Saleeby held that tuberculosis was best
treated through exposure to fresh air and sun and that the bacillus
had less scope for growth outside of crowded urban centres. Arthur

Newsholme, a British eugenist and a specialist on consumption, had written in 1908,

The only statements that can be made ... with absolute certainty are that
  1. Anything favouring an open-air life diminishes tuberculosis.
  2. Tuberculosis is less prevalent in the less densely populated and more isolated communities. (194)[6]

Saleeby pursued what he called the "Imperial implications" of these "certainties," suggesting that these factors existed in abundance in western Canada, making it uniquely conducive to the eradication of the disease: "The cold and sun of Canada, playing upon the well-fed, produce a splendour of physique, a low rate of disease, an abundant energy of mind, a *joie de vivre*, or national *euphoria*" (101), he argued. "Well-fed Canadians, and their superb children not least, are, taken as a whole, the finest people ... anywhere in the world ... They are the most glorious examples of [the] race, and the Dominion they have created is, I believe, the hope of the British Empire" (100). English-Canadians engaged in the work of expansion also believed this and underlined rhetoric like Saleeby's with a stern reminder to immigrants: the "White Man's Last Opportunity" could not be squandered, for at the empire's frontier, the Great North West, the Great White Plague might be cured.

It was into this ideological construction of the Canadian West and the future of the British Empire that McClung introduced her vision of an end to consumption in "the Land of the Second Chance" (1915, 159); and it is this vision that underlies the narrative of the Watson trilogy.[7] Critiques of these novels have emphasized their social reform rhetoric, especially with regard to temperance, and of course the author's involvement in pushing for the vote for white women in Manitoba before 1916 and for prohibition in Alberta in the early 1920s. But tuberculosis and its effects upon the race at the frontiers of the empire also figure, as, indeed, the disease and its effects figure in the temperance and suffrage rhetoric of which McClung is English Canada's primary proponent. It is, in fact, the representation of TB in the series that provides us with a sense of the objectives of McClung's imperial and eugenic feminism. In McClung's narratives of consumption cured we see her situating Canada as the last site for imperial regeneration and at the same time positioning Anglo-colonial women as the "last reserves" in the struggle. The suffragists who took up the cause of "the pollution of the race by infectious diseases like tuberculosis and venereal disease" (Bacchi 1983, 104), along with concerns for the maintenance of western "purity," also suggested that it was women, and especially women at the frontiers of empire, who would lead the race towards that disease's eradication.

Tuberculosis had been designated by Saleeby as a "racial disease" that was, like syphilis, the other "great scourge" of the early twentieth century, a preventable although incurable "poison."[8] The spread of consumption was thus suggestively linked in imperial social reform rhetoric like Saleeby's with the "vicious" spread of sexually transmitted diseases, and the connection persisted for many decades. René and Jean Dubos, for instance, begin their 1952 study *The White Plague* with the statement that tuberculosis is a "social disease" that affects the "social body" (vii). David S. Barnes has analyzed the construction of TB as a "social disease" in nineteenth-century France, where, by 1900, it was "a national scourge, highly contagious, lurking around every corner, and symptomatic of moral decay" (13).

Since moral decay was understood to be symptomatic of imperial decay, tuberculosis came to possess something of the same value as sexually transmitted diseases, and to present itself, like syphilis and gonorrhea, as a cause for reform. By the second decade of the twentieth century, as Richard M. Burke shows, anti-tuberculosis leagues had begun to appear in most imperial nations, including in Canada, where Emily Murphy was a prominent member of the league. In 1920 the International Union against Tuberculosis was founded with headquarters in Geneva (Burke 1938, 58). In England, by 1928, Public Health Law required "a 'TB' scheme to be formed in every county and borough" (58). Feminism, notably, suffrage feminism in English Canada, as Bacchi shows, took up this reform under the banner of women's "concern for the future of the Anglo-Saxon race" and, most significantly, of women's "natural" role as what McClung called "the guardians of the race" (1915, 25).

Since Josephine Butler's campaigns against the Contagious Diseases Acts in the 1870s and '80s, syphilis had been represented as a disease that, while not the exclusive province of men, could be seen to be an effect of "male" vice. Prostitutes, in Butler's reform rhetoric, were not the evil transmitters of disease into the social organism (as the eighteenth-century "harlot" had been, and as many

nineteenth-century accounts continued to suggest)[9] but the hapless
victims of male lust and a patriarchal economy that situated women
as sexual commodities. The Pankhursts, as Lucy Bland and Mariana
Valverde have both pointed out, entrenched the cause of militant
suffragism within an imperialist rhetoric of the destruction visited
upon the race by men. Christabel Pankhurst, as Valverde notes,
"argued that it was men, not women, who were to blame for the
sexual excesses that caused social/racial degeneration ... 'Syphilis is
the prime cause of race degeneration,' Pankhurst stated, criticizing
the gender bias of medical men who blamed prostitutes for venereal
disease while leaving the concept of race degeneration intact"
(1991, 13).[10]

Tuberculosis was not a sexual disease, but when it was bundled
with syphilis as a "racial poison," or a substance that acted through
the individual upon the race, it carried implications for empire that
could readily be exploited in suffrage rhetoric. Here too, that is,
men might be positioned as a major factor in the spread of the
poison, primarily because by the end of the nineteenth century a
connection had been established in medical discourse between TB
and the excessive consumption of alcohol.[11] This connection is a
significant indication of the shift in the representation of the disease
and its increasingly prominent position in imperial social reform
following Koch's discovery of the tubercle bacillus, when it emerged
that consumption was not, as had been thought for much of the
nineteenth century, a disease of heredity but of environment.[12]

Early twentieth-century studies of tuberculosis show that the role
of liquor in the spread of the disease was now seen to be considerable. As one commentator put it, "*L'alcoölisme fait le lit de la
tuberculose*" (Landouzy, cited in Huber 1906, 143). It was "certainly," according to J.B. Huber in his 1906 study, "in a causative
relation ... Pulmonary tuberculosis is almost invariably found in
persons dying in the course of chronic alcoholism" (143). Alcohol
was soon being represented as "the most powerful factor in the
propagation of tuberculosis" (Tri-County, 126), since it affected
both the individual and the domestic environment. Thus to eradicate the one was seen to move towards eliminating the spread of
the other.

Since drinking, like sexual lust, was configured as a male vice,
this connection, while compelling for all social reformers who took
up the anti-tuberculosis cause of the early twentieth century, was

particularly so for feminists. Temperance was an early mainstay of suffrage rhetoric. "Feminists," Bland notes, "cited male alcoholism as a major instigator of men's violence towards women" (1995, 111), and thus a substance that worked against the upward climb of civilization. They also suggested with eugenists such as Saleeby that alcohol sapped the strength of future generations.[13] When suffrage feminists demanded "greater moral 'purity' of male politicians, including a commitment to the aims of temperance" (111), their concerns were primarily eugenical; it was the future of the race that was at stake and that would remain in peril, they implied, as long as men ignored alcohol's dysgenic effects, including tuberculosis. If Canada was to be what imperialist writer Agnes Deans Cameron termed "The Empire of Larger Hope" (*Canada West*, July 1907, 348–56), it was imperative that these pernicious racial poisons be held in check. Under the auspices of suffrage, antituberculosis reform became a crucial part of women's work for empire in the West.[14]

It is this work that is represented in McClung's Watson trilogy, which follows one woman's mission "to serve and save the race." Pearl Watson is an almost messianic figure, Warne has suggested, a "prophet" (1993, 44) leading "her" people to an Edenic West whose salient characteristic is a racial hygiene that must be preserved. This specifically western purity is most tellingly marked in the way that a "cure" for tuberculosis appears after the achievement of woman suffrage and the introduction of the kind of temperance legislation that Pearl preaches in all three novels. Thus, while consumption makes a relatively inauspicious appearance in the first novel, by the second instalment it has gained a position of equal prominence with the temperance question that will, in the third novel, motivate Pearl to take up the cause of woman suffrage. (Pearl, we are told, embraces the cause of enfranchisement only after hearing the minister of education defend the sale of alcohol as "one of our social institutions" [1992, 79].) By the end of *Purple Springs*, with suffrage and temperance secured, tuberculosis and, most importantly, the vision of its cure in the West come to dominate the narrative.

In *Sowing Seeds in Danny* the question of TB, although not as integral to the development of the narrative as it is in *The Second Chance* and *Purple Springs*, nonetheless figures in a significant way in the book's incidental instruction in personal and, consequently, racial hygiene. Pearlie, for example, alludes to bovine tuberculosis and the need to scald well "every drop" of milk (1908, 41–2). At the time McClung published this book, the spread of non-pulmonary consumption through unpasteurized cow's milk was known to be one of the two major means of infection, particularly among children.[15] The other primary means was through "breathing or swallowing the germs" of an infected person. Pearl indicates her awareness of this second danger when she asks Tom Motherwell if his parents will not let him "go near Nellie Slater" because she is "tooberkler" (186). This awareness is also shown in her pleading with Mrs Motherwell to open the window that has been nailed shut in her bedroom. When she informs Mrs Motherwell that she cannot sleep in the room because it is "full of diseases and microscopes" (152) and that they might as well be "in [their] graves" as to keep "the windies all down" (153), Pearl echoes the contemporary medical maxim that "To nail one's bedroom window shut is to drive a nail into one's coffin" (Tri-County, 145). Pearl's references to "tuberoses" in the cows similarly gesture at the presence of the disease in this frontier community. But the novel's real concern about the imperial implications of TB emerges in the sketch of "little" Billy McLean. Billy is identified as "a consumptive," who is "playing a losing game against a relentless foe" (213). His death in the spring is a reminder that the White Plague is at work in the last best West, threatening the work of expansion and regeneration for those whom McClung characterizes in *Purple Springs* as "the real Empire-builders" (1992, 72).[16] Pearlie's advice regarding prevention, we are to perceive, should thus be heeded.

In the second novel in the trilogy, consumption makes an early appearance, with Billy McLean's death echoed in the death of a Watson uncle, also named Bill, also "consumptive" (1910, 29). The disease quickly shifts to the foreground. The story's crisis comes not when alcoholic Bill Cavers, overloaded with drink by the unscrupulous business partner of the bar owner, Sandy Braden, dies in a drunken stupor, but when his daughter Libby Anne develops consumption. Here tuberculosis appears as a result both of genetic predisposition and the deprivation caused by Bill's drinking up the family income. Susceptibility is visited upon Libby Anne just as contemporary manuals of prevention maintained that it would be in such circumstances. The Tri-County Anti-Tuberculosis League in Nova Scotia, for instance, framed the problem in 1911 thus: "As for the children, born and to be born, of the beastly and besotted alcoholic, how can they be expected to inherit a strong and vigorous constitution, or to escape the effects of the sins of their fathers?" (39). As is characteristic of the rhetoric of eugenically minded reform, heredity, while reconfigured here, remains a factor in the spread of the disease. As Karl Pearson put it, "It is not the disease but the diathesis which is inherited, not the seed but the soil" (cited in Burke 1938, 58). For McClung and the western expansionist mission of growing a race, this "soil," as both the new world itself and the imperial social body, was all-important because it *could* be preserved for the empire's "second chance."

Despite the sins of her father, Libby Anne is finally cured; like almost everyone in this novel, she too gets her "second chance" through the work of Pearl. And, just as Libby Anne's infection with tuberculosis is presented as an effect of "King Alcohol," her recovery is concomitantly an effect of the community temperance brought about by Pearl. That is, while she is cured by an operation, it is through the work of the repentant Sandy Braden, converted by Pearl, that the operation takes place at all; he brings the unwilling doctor in the middle of the night in a raging snowstorm. Apart from its association with the resonances of Braden's contrition, however, Libby Anne's "cure" is itself conventional enough. When she is diagnosed with the disease, she is moved outside into a tent. Such tents as these were widely used for consumptives, for whom, even in the province of Manitoba in March, fresh air was believed to be the first and most important medicine.[17] This standard treatment, however, did not always work. Libby Anne, in fact, is saved only by a dramatic midnight operation that suggests the process of collapsing the affected lung that would become popular in the 1930s.[18]

Libby Anne's recovery, like the closing of Sandy Braden's bar, symbolizes through the eradication of these two linked racial poisons the restoration of health to the diseased body of the community. Implicit in this story is a moral message: if temperance and Christian social purity can be maintained in the West through the intervention of women, the regeneration of Anglo-Saxon stock can take place. Tellingly, this novel, like *Sowing Seeds in Danny*, ends with a series of romantic unions. Martha Perkins is joined with the English Arthur Wemyss; Thursa with the shopkeeper Jack Smeaton; and even the newly masculinized prodigal Bud Perkins with "his girl," the recovering Libby Anne. Characteristic of McClung's work, this narrative is best understood as an imperial adventure in racial hygiene, with the significantly female central figure conquering the racial poisons that threaten to pollute the empire's last best West. The end is clearly to be the eugenical reproduction of healthy stock, and it is towards this conclusion that the Watson trilogy has been moving, and that Pearl, the maternal feminist and suffragist, has been leading us.

Purple Springs, the final instalment, begins with a promise of marriage between two figures established from the first novel as "master builders" in the empire, Pearl and the young doctor, Horace Clay (1921c, 104). In *The Second Chance*, as Pearl and Horace tend to Libby Anne in the tent, he tells Pearl that he is going to ask her a question on her nineteenth birthday (1910, 321). *Purple Springs* begins in anticipation of this question. But Horace does not ask Pearl to marry him on her birthday, for on that day he learns that he has tuberculosis. In this third novel, alcohol has moved into the background. Of course, since it is possible that Horace was infected while caring for Libby Anne, alcohol, through Bill Cavers's drinking, is suggestively the "bed" upon which his infection has taken place. But Horace is a temperate man, unlike Dr Barner, whose drunkenness symbolized the community's sorry condition in *Sowing Seeds in Danny*. Drink, moreover, appears to have virtually disappeared from Millford with the closing of Sandy Braden's bar. The children of the Band of Hope with their songs and dramatic presentations about the evils of alcohol do not appear in this novel. However, as Horace's affliction indicates, TB still lingers, the legacy of former intemperance.

In the pattern of contemporary medical commentators who held that no one should marry who did not have a clean bill of health, a view echoed by McClung in much of her own social reform writing, Horace retreats from proposing.[19] ("The careful consumptive," as the Tri-County Anti-Tuberculosis League darkly suggests, "sleeps alone" [1911, 122].) Pearl, meanwhile, takes up schoolteaching and pursues the women's suffrage cause. In this work, she meets a woman, Annie Graham, who has been ostracized by the people in the community because they believe her to be an unwed mother. Annie's name is an assumed one and serves to hide her and her child from her father-in-law (who is, in the novel, the premier of Manitoba). Annie has named her retreat "Purple Springs" to obscure the real Purple Springs, a valley that Annie's late husband had discovered in the northern part of the province, and, ultimately, the novel's key to imperial regeneration.

"We found out," Annie tells Pearl, "that the water in the streams had healing power ... [The Indians] brought their sick children and their old people, and the results were marvelous. I never knew the stream to fail" (1921c, 258). The restorative effects of the springs are, moreover, also specific to the problem of consumption that is keeping Pearl and Horace apart. "Even the tubercular people soon began to grow rosy and well," Annie continues. "The food seemed to have healing power, too, and some who came hollow-cheeked, feverish, choking with their cruel paroxysms of coughing, soon began to grow fat and healthy" (258). When Annie comes out of hiding after the Conservative premier is displaced – through Pearl's performance in the Women's Parliament – by the pro-woman suffrage and pro-temperance Liberals, she brings with her the promise of a cure for consumption that far exceeds the conventional measures undertaken in *The Second Chance*.[20] Since tuberculosis functions in *Purple Springs* as the primary hindrance to the progress of imperial regeneration, it is this prospect of a cure that provides the happy ending of McClung's series.

With Pearl and Horace finally united, we see the two poised on the brink of what is configured as a new day in a new world where "old world" diseases no longer have any power. They sit, "hand-in-hand, with the glory of the sunset transfiguring the every-day world, [while] Pearl t[ells] Horace of the wonder valley of hot springs in the far North, whose streams have magical powers of healing. The valley of Purple Springs – away beyond the sunset" (330–1). Pearl has no doubt that Horace will be cured by the healing waters. We are not to have any doubts of his recovery either, for Pearl and Horace make their "covenant" here, and such a union would otherwise not be condoned in McClung's didactic work.

The romance of Pearl and Horace is a story of imperial regeneration through white woman suffrage, for it is Pearlie's successful leadership of the push for female enfranchisement in Manitoba that leads to a cure for Horace. McClung's message is clear: only when women have a say in the laws that affect them will the way be opened up to the kind of renewal that Purple Springs offers. The last best West, in other words, has a promise of purifying regeneration for the empire's weakening stock, but only women can lead the way and save the race. Indeed, not just any woman can undertake this work

– only, as the editor who praises Pearl in the Millford *Mercury*
makes explicit, the reconfigured imperial and maternal New Woman
(115) – a messiah of racial hygiene.

The vision of a natural Canadian cure for tuberculosis makes
Purple Springs a significant story of race renewal in the Canadian
West. Before the appearance in the 1940s of antibiotics such as
streptomycin, the only hope for the eradication of the racial poison
seen to be decimating Anglo-Saxondom was prevention. As Saleeby
put it in 1924, the "tubercle bacillus is 'the cause' of tuberculosis,
but so also is the susceptibility of the patient. Toxicity is not in the
poison alone but in the poisonableness of the poisoned. We must
neglect no means" (176). The Watson trilogy outlines such
"means." Woman suffrage, as Pearl represents it, was thus not an
end in itself but a remedy invoked "in times like these" when masculine governance and war were seen to have brought the imperial
race to the brink of disaster.

7

"In a Chinese Restaurant,
Working at Night"
Painted Fires, White Slavery, and the
Protection of the Imperial Mother

"It's quare to be livin' in a country where the whole world comes to
see us," Maggie thought to herself when two Hindus with their lightly
draped head-dress walked haughtily by, followed by a colored man and
woman with their little girl held by the hand.

"I'm glad I'm white," said Maggie to herself; "a white skin may be
harder to keep clean, but it's worth the trouble."

McClung, *Painted Fires*

Painted Fires, Nellie McClung's fourth and final novel, has usually
been regarded, as she herself designated the book, as an "immigration story" (1945, 237). Published in 1925 but set in the years
before and during World War I, it is the story of a Finnish girl,
Helmi Milander, and her "discovery" of a "new" nation far different from the land of opportunity represented in the immigrationist
propaganda generated by Prime Minister Wilfred Laurier's government for the purposes of peopling the Canadian West. The "streamlining" of immigration policy by Minister of the Interior Clifford
Sifton, Howard Palmer has suggested, had created considerable tension in the Anglo-Canadian western settler culture, whose response
to the "arrival of hundreds of thousands of newcomers from around
the globe" (1982, 22) before the war was increasingly nativist and
concerned with the protection of the imperial "race" in the West.[21]
This response had been articulated in 1909 by James S. Woodsworth,
who complained in his *Strangers within Our Gates* that the Canadian "progressive immigration policy," while bringing "a large

number of Britishers," also brought "immigrants from all parts of
Europe": "We are taking our place, side by side with the United
States as the Old World's dumping ground" (165–6). Concern
about the effect of incoming non-Anglo-Saxons on the English-
Canadian population rose sharply after the war. Reconstruction
publications with titles such as *The New Era in Canada* (1917) and
*The Birthright: A Search for the Canadian Canadian and the Larger
Loyalty* (1919) configured the "strain of the times" (Hawkes, n.p.)
as a racial question rooted in the "problem" of immigration.

Painted Fires, in its account of Helmi's overcoming a series of
hazards from male sexual "prospecting" to a racist social bureaucracy, highlights McClung's own ambivalent position with regard
to an open-door immigration policy and its perceived effects upon
the race. McClung clearly supported the idea that Canada "need[ed]
people" ("Eighth Day," 1921, 259) but only, as she made clear on
several occasions, if newcomers were filtered through a system of
benevolent naturalization.[22] While, that is, she welcomed "people
who come to us from other countries" ("Naturalization," *Western
Home Monthly,* October 1921, 3), she also maintained that there
was a pressing need for the assimilative processes of "Christianizing
and Canadianizing" non-Anglo-Saxon immigrants.[23] *Painted Fires*
worked to reaffirm prevailing imperialist racial hierarchies by
making a case for the importance of the "uplift" of putatively
"lower" races, at the same time as it purported to expose "the false
flattery which has been given to our country by immigration agen-
cies in Europe anxious to bring out settlers for the profit of steamship
and railway companies" (1945, 241).[24]

Critics (Harrison, Roberts, Warne) along with historians and
sociologists (Palmer, Valverde) have tended to favour this latter
reading, which, after all, is authorized by McClung in her autobiography. She maintains there that she wrote the book to "lay down
a hard foundation of truth as to conditions in Canada" (1945, 241).
However, since the novel does not notably disturb the propagan-
dists' representation of Canada, as a young L.M. Montgomery put
it in an 1891 article in the *Prince Albert Times,* as a "Western Eden"
where "earnest toil will be ... abundantly rewarded" (17 June 1891,
4), it is difficult to pinpoint what precisely is being represented as
the "truth" whose exposure is McClung's professed object. *Painted
Fires* clearly supports the idea of the "Western Eden," the Englishman Arthur Warner's assertion "that any man should be able to

wrest a living from the soil if he had a dog for company, an axe, a gun and few seeds" (1925, 192). Warner, who begins by cultivating "a piece of land for his garden with a wooden hoe of his own making" (192) and spends the winters trapping, within a few years has "built a shingled bungalow, with glassed-in verandah, and hardwood floors" (193). Helmi similarly "wrests" fruit from the soil; her little garden serves, like Warner's house, as a sign that hard work will be rewarded in the Canadian West. Her "head-lettuce, radishes, onions, cabbage, carrots, and beets" grow "beautifully" and earn her "twenty-four dollars" (204–5). Her discovery of a seam of "high-grade anthracite" on the land she inherits from Warner is an even more compelling advertisement for the promise of the Land of the Second Chance (1915, 159).

The truth that *Painted Fires* purports to expose thus does not have to do with the idea of western Canada as a land of opportunity. Indeed, while it may be possible to see the narrative initially working against the propagandist representation of a "country where prosperity and freedom are awaiting thousands, a country where all may be happy and equal" (Montgomery 1891, 4), it is precisely this notion that the romantic conclusion reinforces. McClung's closing scene shows the hero and heroine finally united and surrounded by their "happy group of children and collie dogs" (1925, 333). Clustered around their "large gray stucco home" are the signs of their mining community's prosperity and happiness. This model settlement boasts a "green and white bath-house," a "recreation ground," and a "white church," a "club-house for the miners and their wives," and a "well appointed dining-room" for the boys' and girls' clubs (333). The community's cleanliness is signalled in the bath-house, its godliness in the church, its commitment to healthy living in the recreation ground, its equality in the suggestion that these areas are open to all.

This pastoral scene appears to function as an optimistic realization of the ideal McClung had delineated in 1915 as "the land of the Fair Deal, where every race, color and creed will be given exactly the same chance" (1915, 158). However, it also reminds us of what is obscured by the critical tendency to situate this novel only in relation to misleading propaganda, and thus to incoming "Canadians-to-be." That is, the impetus behind the "immigration story" of *Painted Fires* was not only to expose the "dark tragedy" McClung saw visited upon newcomers "deceived" by "false flattery" (1945,

241) but to promote the effective integration of "foreigners" into an Anglo-Saxon culture. Woodsworth had suggested that the great "problem" of immigration into Canada was "to show how the incoming tides of immigrants of various nationalities and different degrees of civilization may be assimilated and made worthy citizens of the great Commonwealths" (7). *Painted Fires* takes up this problem: its story traces the successful assimilation of Helmi Milander into Saxondom, as it also shows how she, like Pearl Watson, is one of the women whom McClung saw as English Canada's – and the empire's – last best hope for renewal.

Marilyn Hallett and Mary Davis have argued that McClung's "immigration story" differs from the kind of law-and-order narrative being produced in the years before the war by writers such as Ralph Connor. Hallett and Davis follow E.L. Bobak in suggesting that *Painted Fires* is *not* like Connor's 1909 assimilationist novel, *The Foreigner*, because here "we will find not so much an overemphasis on the Canadianizing of the new-comer ... but an emphasis on the 'Finnizing' of Canadian women" (Bobak, 85–6, cited in Davis and Hallett, 1994, 251). "This," they claim, "sets McClung's heroine apart from Connor's foreigner who is shaped by the West" (251). But the story *is* concerned with the Canadianizing of the newcomer. While, that is, Helmi is represented as the kind of woman McClung saw as the "white hope" for the race, she is also, we are to see, in need of a "hand up" if she is to function as the centre of a healthy community (1945, 182). Initially she does not speak English, and she has a temper that is configured as an undesirable "racial" characteristic. Moreover, her Christianity is represented as being fundamentally primitive.[25] The God she brings with her from the Old World is a "terrible person" who "looked down with terrible burning eyes, seeing everything from His white throne in the sky, and [able to] wither bad people with one scorching blast" (1925, 49). Helmi sees God as having enacted such vengeful justice upon a neighbour in Finland, "found blackened and dead beside his plow, though his horses were not touched, just because he had cheated the storekeeper" (49). *Painted Fires* traces Helmi's "upward" movement in learning to speak English, to control her temper, and to comprehend "true" Christianity ("They ... have a nice God in Canada" [50.]) This, the novel intimates, is the path that leads to the kind of happiness we see at the end of the story,

for Helmi and for the community, both immediate and, in the sense
suggested by Benedict Anderson, imagined as nation.

Nonetheless, as Davis and Hallett indicate, McClung's "immigrant
story" differs from Connor's account of the neutralizing of "foreigners" through the strong hand of Anglo-Celtic law. Although in
one sense Helmi is as "foreign" as Connor's Galicians, she also
belongs to a racialized category represented in early twentieth-
century rhetoric of immigration as the most desirable of all non-
Anglo-Saxon immigrants.[26] Woodsworth, for instance, classified
Scandinavians, amongst whom he included Finns, first among the
"strangers" he ranked in his 1909 study (74). "Taken all in all,"
he wrote, "there is no class of immigrants that are as certain of
making their way in the Canadian West as the people of the pen-
insula of Scandinavia. Accustomed to the rigors of a northern climate, clean-blooded, thrifty, ambitious and hard-working, they will
be certain of success in this pioneer country, where the strong, not
the weak, are wanted" (77).

According to Woodsworth, a group of Swedish farmers might
easily "pass" for "a meeting of Scotch settlers" – "serious, thought-
ful, sober, determined and possibly a little bit obstinate" (74). What,
in his view, made Scandinavians so desirable to the nation was not
only their ability to "pass" as Celts, but their perceived ability to
integrate: "They easily assimilate with the Anglo-Saxon peoples,
and readily intermarry, so that they do not form isolated colonies
as do other European immigrants" (76), such, Connor suggests, as
"Galicians." It is this ideal of assimilation that is rehearsed in the
mining community at the end of *Painted Fires*. Finnish Helmi has
married Anglo-Canadian Jack Doran; together they have produced
a "happy group of children" (1925, 333); and, while there is a
"Finnish bath-house," this is a definitively Anglo-Saxon community,
located as it is, "on the bank of English River" (333).

The bath-house, in its juxtaposition with the white church and
the recreation ground, is an image that hints at the eugenic interests
of this novel. The concluding tableau serves as a reminder that one
objective of *Painted Fires* is to suggest that selected racial characteristics imported to the nation may, through careful assimilation
and intermarriage, serve the Anglo-Saxon race in good stead. Thus,
what is presented as the "natural" tendency of Finns to be "neat
and clean" (25) is also suggested to be a hereditarian infusion of

some value to the nation.[27] Helmi's own cleanliness, like Pearl Watson's, is insistently foregrounded in the narrative, configured in marked contrast to the slovenliness of "Cockney" Martha. The point of the account of Helmi's violent response to Martha's sorry dishwashing habits in the kitchen of her first workplace is not only to draw attention to Helmi's "Finnish" temper but to indicate that Martha's "British tradition" – that "foreigners were dirty and ignorant, and 'certainly could tell her nothink'" (23) – could usefully be displaced by Helmi's similarly racialized sense of hygiene, without, however, fundamentally altering Anglo-imperial dominance.

If Helmi's impulse to clean is represented, like her "high temper," as something that inheres as essence in her "Finnishness" and makes her a "desirable" immigrant, it is also a characteristic that we are to see as having been transmitted along gendered lines. It is Finnish *women* whom McClung portrays as naturally "neat and clean." When, for instance, Helmi sees a grubby, disordered family on the train, "the spirit of [her] hard-working, soap-making, dirt-hating grandmothers stirred at the sight before her. Her long, capable hands craved a chance to show what they could do with the travel-stained, tear-wet, much begrimed family before her, mother and all" (121). That it is Helmi's "grandmothers" who have bequeathed this characteristic to her is a significant reminder of the novel's embedding in the politics of eugenic feminism, which saw the "natural" inclinations of women to clean and "mother" ideally enacted not only upon their own families but upon the race as a whole. As with Martha and the dishes, the implication in Helmi's cleaning of the family, "mother and all," is that this Finnish girl has something valuable to bring to the nation, if she could be enabled to put her "capable hands" to the kind of imperial reform work that McClung configured as a woman-powered social and moral "housecleaning" (1915, 166).

In McClung's feminism, gender, if it did not necessarily ever transcend race as a category of identification, was nonetheless seen to link women and women's work across racial as well as class boundaries.[28] For instance, in 1915 McClung pointedly aligned Anglo-imperial women in Canada with German women when she suggested that "women with boys of their own would [n]ever sit down and wilfully plan slaughter" (143). This argument is the basis for McClung's suffrage contention that it had become crucial for women to be enfranchised to counter the dysgenic effects of "male statecraft" (143). It is also an indication of her perception of gender as essence, and of femaleness, across race, as characterized by maternalism. It might thus be argued that the Canadianized Helmi of the conclusion does not so much "Finnize" Canadian women as she "McClungizes" them, for "Finnish" cleanliness is only one element of Helmi's work. What she brings to the community – indeed, what shapes it – is the kind of maternal instinct that is also the salient feature of Pearlie Watson, Maggie Corbett, and all the model empire-building women in McClung's fiction.

Like Pearlie, Helmi is defined by what is represented as her innate maternalism. Even at seventeen, Helmi is shown to be physically and emotionally geared towards what McClung maintained were women's two "natural" duties: childbearing and the extension of domestic care to moral reform. Helmi has, we are told, an "ample form" (39), that, while distasteful to her, is contrasted favourably to the "extreme slimness" of the childless and dysgenically inclined opium addict Eva St John. In addition, moreover, to "the large, restless hands which generations of hard-working women acquire, eager, capable, hands ready for anything that has to be done" (1925, 27), Helmi has inherited what we are to see is a wholesome sense of her future role. When Jack reprimands her for artlessly observing that, because his house is close to the river, "kids might fall in" (148), she remains "grave and unabashed. Generations of child-bearing women whose business in life was the rearing and protection of their young had spoken through her" (149).

Helmi's overt suitability for motherhood is reinforced in the representation of her own desire to have children, which, according to McClung, "every normal woman" wanted (1915, 25). Although her romantic fantasy is to meet and marry a prospector (28) (as she does), her "real" hope for the future is to marry and have children. This hope is crystallized when she is en route from Winnipeg to Eagle Mines and sees "the station family" at supper: "A rosy lamp with a wide umbrella threw a circle of mellow light over the table. Helmi could see the father helping macaroni and cheese from a large white bowl. A baby sat in his high-chair pounding impatiently on a blue enamel plate, a girl about Helmi's age, in a white middy, sat beside him; Helmi wondered if that girl knew it was nice to have a family of your own, even if you did have to look after the baby and clean the messy tray of his high-chair after every meal" (1925, 119). This early emphasis on Helmi's maternalism suggests that we are to see the novel's already potentially assimilable Finnish heroine as a future imperial mother, her value to the nation situated both in her "capable hands" and the promise of her womb.

In a weightily symbolic scene, Helmi's maternal role in relation to Anglo-Saxondom is established with the birth of her child. Alone, almost penniless, believing herself the dupe of both her husband, Jack, who is overseas fighting, and the magistrate who had not wanted to marry them, Helmi gives birth on Christmas Eve at the North Star Rooming House. She is attended by Maggie Corbett (the "finger-post" heroine of *The Black Creek Stopping-House*) and a tenant of the house, Mrs Kalinski, described by Maggie as a "good Christian ... though she is a Jew" (220). Mrs Kalinski, who is "expectin' her own trouble," brings Helmi "her own little basket with the dotted muslin over the blue sateen, and everything in it that [was] needed, the burnt linen and all" (220). The suggested association of Helmi with the Virgin Mary is made explicit when Rose and Danny Corbett, on their way to the Salvation Army Cantata, sing, "Away in a manger, no crib for a bed,/ The little Lord Jesus laid down His sweet head." Their carol brings "to Helmi's mind the Christmas story; and because her own heart was more tender than it had ever been, owing to the rise and fall of the little white veil which covered Lili's face, she loved the little Christ Child more than ever, and thought of Him and His pale mother as they lay there in the manger with the noise of cattle all around them" (229).

Helmi emerges here as a supreme mother of the race, indeed, with Maggie Corbett in *The Black Creek Stopping-House* and Mrs Burton in *Sowing Seeds in Danny*, a veritable new-world madonna, whose child, Lili, in this case, carries the future promise of the race. On the one hand a step in the narrative process of Helmi's uplifting conversion to the religion of the "nice God in Canada," this scene also establishes Helmi's importance to the country as a bearer of its children. What, in effect, is played out here is a tableau of feminist nation-building, with three fundamentally maternal women gathering together, despite what are represented as racial differences, to facilitate the birth of a child whose function as a "white hope" is conveyed by her name.

Implicit in this representation of the birth of the new Lili is the suggestion that Helmi, like Pearlie Watson, is possessed of the potential to lead the race into the light of a regenerative new day, such as we see in the mining community at the end of the novel. Helmi is described then as someone who holds the community together by uniting its women with a kind of super-maternal power, making the women "band together," as McClung's ideal eugenic feminist should. "The hearts of the women," we are told, "were knitted to Helmi's because she had a way of comforting them in their troubles. There was a strength in the touch of her hand, and healing in her presence" (332). As a future mother of the race, Helmi would be a national asset. As the super-mother we see at the Christmas birth and in the conclusion, she is an asset of what McClung would have us understand is immense value. This is emphasized in the novel's insistent alignment of the "fiery gold" of her hair with the gold as natural resource for which so many men in the book are prospecting. We are, in fact, to see Helmi as the "real" gold of the narrative, as we see when Jack tells her that he does not need to look for gold anymore: he got his gold, he says, "from Finland" (333).

The representation of Helmi as a natural resource and a national asset for English Canada indicates that *Painted Fires* is telling an "immigration story" that is concerned as much with the preservation of the Anglo-Saxon race as with the treatment of "newcomers." Helmi is clearly one of the ideal "mother-women" whom McClung argued in *In Times Like These* were needed "to serve and save the race" by bearing its children and working for moral and social reform. This novel follows Woodsworth in promoting the idea that Scandinavians were especially desirable because they "easily assimilate" and "readily intermarry" (Woodsworth 1909, 76). It supplements this idea with a suggestion that the cleanliness Helmi possesses as an aspect of her "Finnishness" and her well-developed race- and gender-based maternal instinct, are attributes that, through intermarriage with good Anglo-Canadian stock, would infuse the race with the kind of characteristics needed to preserve the West as an imperial space and a location for Anglo-Saxon renewal. Helmi, that is, is to serve the positive eugenic purpose of breeding in good qualities and thus ensuring the improvement of the race without disturbing its Anglo-Saxonness – or, crucially, as the foregrounding of Helmi's "creamy skin" (1925, 40) reminds us, its whiteness.

If *Painted Fires* demonstrates a profound racial anxiety in its concern with the eugenical preservation of Anglo-Saxondom from incoming "tides" of "foreigners" through assimilation and maternal feminist reform, it also conveys a deep sexual anxiety in its suggestion that the women thought to be needed to serve and save the new world were themselves in need of protection. *Painted Fires* thus differs from McClung's earlier narratives not so much in its presentation of the future imperial regenerator as a woman who has come from *outside* the British Empire (Helmi, after all, is successfully assimilated, and even indigenized: she is "as sweet and pure as a prairie flower" [1925, 166]) but in its suggestion that what Saleeby called "the eugenic prospect" was imperilled by the failure of white Canadian "race culture" to pay attention to its incoming breeding stock. The narrative of Helmi's "uplift" and her "value" is thus underscored by a cautionary tale that works to show the future of the race to be compromised by the sexual exploitation of its future mothers.

Helmi is confronted at every turn by sexual danger. From the moment she arrives and finds her Aunt Lili dying of consumption, she is threatened by men whom we are to see as new-world opportunists, sexual "prospectors" who "just want their own pleasure" (11). "Men are so bad, and it's hard for a young girl alone," Helmi's Aunt Lili warns her, hoping that she will return to Finland. Canada is "a good country, but it's too hard for a pretty girl who has no English" (12). Lili's advice is immediately put to work: at her funeral, her abusive husband (he has beaten her with a chair) "pinched [Helmi's] arm affectionately ... and told her to call him 'Mike' and cut the 'Uncle' stuff. His burning eyes made her shudder" (12). When Mike fails to snare Helmi, largely through the intervention of the female kitchen staff, he comforts himself with the observation that Helmi still faces a good deal of danger from men: "A girl like that, right off the farm in Finnland [sic], with a pretty face and no English – Some fellow would be too smart for her" (13).

Helmi's next "narrow escape" is similarly sexual. Sitting on a hill, dreaming "that she might some day meet a prospector ... who had found gold" (28), she does not notice the approach of two young men.

They were close upon her when she looked up. She did not like their appearance ...

They said something to her in English.

"Yes," she said, because it was the only word she could think of – and then added – "No talk – Finn."

The boys laughed at that and looked at each other meaningly. (28–9)

The question the two men ask evidently has to do with a sexual exchange. They choose to interpret her "yes" as consent and pursue her. Helmi escapes by giving the first "a powerful body blow which sent him rolling down the bank towards the stream below" (29), her physical strength matching, and, it is implied, demonstrating her moral rectitude. Nonetheless, she *is* in danger, and is "rescued" by Miss Abbie Moore, a spinster of the kind McClung so frequently represented, precisely through rescue work of this nature, as one of the potential mothers of the race. Miss Abbie undertakes Helmi's "uplift," unofficially adopting her; but she cannot protect her from the forces at work threatening Helmi's maternal promise to the nation. As we might surmise when we see Helmi installed in a room and sleeping under "a patched [quilt] of blue and white, in the pattern known as the 'Pavements of New York'" (35), the threat of prostitution for women seeking adventure in the New World is always very near. Early twentieth-century accounts of the "white slave trade" – the entrapment of white girls or women for the purposes of prostitution – commonly configured the "immigrant girl" as particularly vulnerable to schemes devised by predators to lure innocent girls into brothels.[29] *Painted Fires* reminds its readers of what was, by 1925, an "immigration story" that had been told again and again in reform rhetoric, significantly juxtaposing the narrative of Helmi's "uplift" with a tale whose dramatic effect derives from its appearing to show her "fall."

The concept of white slavery that by the first decade of the twentieth century had been dramatically brought to public attention by W.T. Stead's 1885 series of articles in the *Pall Mall Gazette* was at the centre of a moral panic which, while it crossed national boundaries, was always an imperial issue.[30] That is, it was in the context of imperial expansionism and its attendant anxieties about reproduction and power that the white slave emerged as the exploited obverse of the white woman as mother of the race – not so much a "common" prostitute as a figure of ordinary womanhood who represented the possibility of plundered reproductive stock.[31] The fear that Britain's women were being sold into sexual slavery abroad was exacerbated by the increased mobility of women around the globe, precisely *for* the purpose of reproducing the race. In North America, in both the United States and Canada, where there was a strong sense of building new Anglo-Saxon nations, the fear was that these women would disappear before a strong new country could develop. American journalist George Kibbe Turner put it thus in a 1907 report in *McClure's* magazine on vice in the city of Chicago: "The chastity of woman is at the foundation of Anglo-Saxon society. Our laws are based upon it, and the finest and most binding of our social relations. Nothing could be more menacing to a civilization than the sale of this as a commodity" (April 1907: 582).

In 1915 in *In Times Like These*, McClung had suggested that white slavery, like alcohol, was an index of male immorality and the effects it had on the nation as long as it remained "unchecked" (24). The white slave traffic, along with the liquor traffic, served as evidence of the adverse effects of what McClung called "too much masculinity." If not a racial poison per se, it was certainly seen to be a method for the transportation of poisons (venereal disease, alcohol, tuberculosis) into "the race." "Do women wish for these things?" McClung asked, "Do the gentle mothers whose hands [we are told] rule the world declare in favor of these things?" (25). Since, of course, as other first-wave feminists such as Christabel Pankhurst and Elizabeth Robins demonstrated, they did not, it was necessary for the "gentle mothers" to take up the cause, as McClung does in *Painted Fires*. McClung's novel is not a "white slave narrative" in the style of Elizabeth Robins's 1913 *Where Are You Going To ...?*, which tells the story of a young British girl tricked from her home and lost forever into what is implied as sexual slavery, but it does nonetheless make considerable use of the conventions of the genre.

The pitfalls that Helmi meets would certainly be familiar to contemporary readers as the stock-in-trade of the white slave narratives that proliferated in North America and the British Empire in the years of expansionism and immigration. She arrives alone with minimal facility in English. Her only relative immediately dies. Her aunt's evil husband attempts to seduce her at the funeral. She works first in a hotel, then in a mining camp, the first a public place, and a likely spot for men to exploit poor and vulnerable young girls, the second made notorious in North America after an early century WCTU publication "exposing" white slavery in Minnesota lumber camps.[32] She is threatened with rape by two men. She becomes the dupe of the opium addicted middle-class woman Eva St John. She goes first to a jail, where she encounters prostitutes, then to a girls' reform school, where she lives with young "fallen" women. She agrees to marry a man about whom she knows nothing.

And, perhaps most significantly for North Americans on the look-out for signs of white slavery in the first quarter of the century, she works in a Chinese restaurant.

From the beginning, Helmi is established as the kind of girl who might easily fall prey to sexual prospectors. Although we see her to be pure and stalwart, we are also to see that, in addition to her new immigrant status and her obvious "foreignness" and aloneness, she has what could easily be a fatal weakness. Helmi exhibits a fascination with luxury and dress, a characteristic that was regarded as a snare for girls and as a moral weakness that would let them fall easily into the hands of procurers. Ernest A. Bell, for instance, editor of the 1910 collection *War on the White Slave Trade*, "after conversing with many thousands of fallen women and misguided girls," argued that one of "the principal causes of their downfall" is "wilfulness and love of ease and finery" (1925, 240). Helmi loves to dress up, and admires Eva St John primarily because of her elegant clothes and beautiful home.

Miss Abbie, who rescues Helmi from the two young men early in the novel, sees this dangerous characteristic and attempts to nip it in the bud (36–7). But it remains at first almost as prominent in the representation of Helmi as her whiteness and her fiery temper. Helmi is put at risk right away by the caprice of Eva St John, who indulgently dresses her in a silk gown for a party: "The whole air around her, the chaste, unimpeachable air of Miss Abbie's kitchen, trembled and glittered with visions. Her little world had been suddenly changed by the touch of clinging silks and the gleam of starry eyes – and those were her own! Her young soul was intoxicated with the new wine of beauty and adventure" (57). The juxtaposition of this "new" world of sexual danger with the "chaste, unimpeachable" air of Miss Abbie's kitchen is telling: Helmi is being presented with two possible kinds of "adventure," and she must choose the right one if she – along with the nation, the empire, and the race – are to be saved.

Although there is no shortage in this novel of "bad" men who ensnare young girls, it is Eva St John who is the real villain of the story. Her work to serve herself and ruin Helmi shows her to be deeply infected with "parasitism," as Charlotte Perkins Gilman would put it, and thus, as McClung had argued in *In Times Like These*, the greatest hazard for the race and a "herald" of its decline (100). Eva is married to a doctor and therefore, in McClung's

vocabulary of representation, ought to serve as a leader of moral
and social hygiene. But she is addicted to opium, a narcotic and
another "racial poison," and, crucially, a problem being widely discussed in Canada. In 1922, Emily Murphy published *Black Candle*,
her account of the drug trade in Canada, based on a series of articles
she had written for *Maclean's* in the early 1920s. The book
described the extent of the traffic and urged Canadians to counter
it before it had a pervasively detrimental effect upon the race.

Helmi, who has begun her process of assimilation through doing
housework for Miss Abbie, learning Canadian "values" through
the Girls' Friendly Society, and studying English with Eva St John,
arrives one day for her lesson (the irony is obvious) to find "her
lovely lady lying with face white and drawn, her eyes burning like
Aunt Lili's had been," in "a darkened room, smelling heavily of
some strange odor" (1925, 60). The racial poisons and racial diseases are presented with the same effect upon the body: Aunt Lili's
tuberculosis and Eva's drug use both produce "burning" eyes, an
effect that is also evident in men such as Mike who show signs of
racially toxic moral degeneracy. Telling her that she needs special
medicine, Eva sends Helmi to the Chinese restaurant, the Shanghai
Chop Suey House, where she obtains her drug. Thus Eva, instead
of protecting Helmi, sends her down the path of what, in a
conventional white slave narrative, would be her inevitable fall.

The restaurant is clearly a portal to danger: "The name was on
the door in gold and red – foreign looking letters with many sharp
points" (62). When Helmi enters, she finds the room "strangely
cold and dead" but filled with writhing serpents, an image regularly
deployed in North American representations of Oriental danger in
this period. Charles Shepherd, for instance, in his "account" of
Chinese sexual slave girls, *The Ways of Ah Sin* (1923), configures
the girls as having landed "in the coils of the serpent." Similarly,
Sam, the man Helmi encounters at the restaurant, is represented
through snake-like imagery: "His ghastly yellow hands had claw-
like nails that seemed to twist around her hand as she took [the
box of opium]." "You nice liddle girl," he says, " – you come see
pretty things – old Sam show you – maybe" (63).

Before she can escape from Sam's clutches, however, she is caught
in a drug raid and thrown into jail. The way down is opened to
her again in the holding cell she shares with two prostitutes. "A
nice young girl, smart and spunky, would be 'andy for us now,"

observes one woman (like slatternly dishwashing Martha, a McClungian specimen of undesirable Anglo-Saxonness), "and 'ere's the place to get them. I got Clara here, you mind, and she was a grand girl to me till the Harmy [the Salvation Army] got 'er and turned 'er against me. Poor Clara, she's a roustabout now in some-one's kitchen, and that girl 'ad 'er silks and 'er satins with me" (71–2). "I'll have a go with the new little girl and try to win her over," says her companion (72). "They always fight at first" (71).

Helmi is convicted of attempting to obtain illegal drugs, largely, we are to see, because she is "foreign" and because she is wrongly associated by the magistrate with another Finnish girl, Anna Milander, who had been arrested at a labour demonstration the week before. Helmi is sent to the Girls' Friendly Home which "stands on a hill overlooking the city": "It seemed to be ever looking down with its many eyes on the struggling people below, watching them with kindly glances, ever beckoning to those who are sore beset in the struggle to come up and find safety" (79). McClung's Girls' Home is reminiscent of "The House on the Hill" in Shepherd's *The Ways of Ah Sin*. In his book, Miss McCormack, who, we are pointedly told, "rejoiced in a heritage of splendid ancestry, which stood out all over her, and found expression in every move" (67), had "for more than a score of years ... been engaged at the task of rescuing Chinese slave girls; and during that time over fifteen hundred girls had been snatched from the hands of ruthless owners and given refuge in that haven of safety, 'The House on the Hill'" (68). While, in Shepherd's account, the hand of the law is benevolent and just, in McClung's there is a considerable degree of what she always describes as "male statecraft" (1915, 143) at work in what she represents as the corrupt Canadian system. The magistrate who convicts her is shown to be unjust, and the couple who run the Home are clearly "iniquitous" (1925, 76). The magistrate who later reluctantly marries Helmi and Jack is also "bad," his dirty house and drinking habits serving to show how he is a factor in the poisoning of the race in the otherwise pristine and promising new West. "You don't need to marry this girl," he tells Jack. "These foreigners are not particular – this license will do her. They have great respect for a paper, and a man of your standing will soon tire of a girl who has nothing but a pretty face" (164).

If *Painted Fires* is at one level concerned with revealing the "truth" about Canada for immigrants, its critique inheres in its focus on the problems of the "masculine" system rather than on the promise of the nation itself. McClung, in fact, indicates in her autobiography that she is concerned with problems specific to new *female* immigrants, not in the account of her motivation in writing the novel but in a story that precedes this account, of Emil Milander, a Finnish man visiting McClung's Finnish maid. At first, she writes, she is "somewhat doubtful of this fine-looking gentleman in the blue suit": "I knew from past experience that foreign girls have often been bitterly deceived by their own countrymen in Canada who shamelessly take advantage of the girls' ignorance of our laws. I knew one girl who believed she was legally married because her countryman had shown her a 'paper' and told her that was all that was needed in Canada. The paper turned out to be an overdue tax notice" (238).

McClung's suggestion that "foreign girls" were likely to be deceived by "their own countrymen" had its basis in claims made that since the early years of the century the cities of the New World were the centres of sexual commerce operated by "foreigners" who imported girls from their own nations, as well as exporting Anglo-Saxon girls to sexual markets abroad. Here too McClung is arguably less concerned with the protection of Anglo-Saxon Canada from "Promiscuous Foreign Immigration" (Palmer, 22) than with the protection of the future "mothers of the race" from "promiscuous" men, who had, she suggests, manipulated the system in the New World and were rapidly leading it towards the same degeneracy that was seen to afflict the Old World.

Protecting Helmi is the crucial work of the novel, because she has the ability, based on her racial and gendered characteristics, to serve and save the race. McClung draws attention to the importance of changing the system, and to the role of women in its change or, as in the case of the parasitic Eva St John, its detrimental sustenance. It is the group of "mother-women" whose interventions help Helmi through the sexual hazards strewn in her path; the Girls' Friendly Society leads her in the right direction towards the nation that could be, as long as male statecraft is successfully countered by women; Helmi's own indefatigable virtue keeps her from corruption. *Painted Fires* is a polemical novel: like the Watson trilogy, which takes on the question of women's work to cure the diseased body of empire, it makes the point that, if there were to be continued imperial – or *racial* – advance, it could only happen with "the work and the help of the women." But *Painted Fires* supplements the Watson trilogy's "politico-propagandist" message (Logan and French 1924, 303) with an argument that the women themselves needed to be both empowered and protected, if they were to do the work that Helmi's story suggests was still so badly needed in the West. This protection, the novel suggests. needed to be undertaken by women themselves rather than by men, many of whom, according to McClung, were interested in protecting their own interests and exploiting girls through the system of male statecraft.

McClung's eugenic feminist work in *Painted Fires* is perhaps most compellingly coded in her ambivalent representation of the Chinese restaurant. The site for a young white woman's encounter with substances or circumstances that would adversely affect the quality of the race (opium, prostitution, miscegenation), it is also the only place where Helmi can find work after she has had her baby and must support herself in Jack's absence. Where the "bad" Chinese Sam dispensing drugs at the beginning of the novel clutches her with his claw-like hand, the "better" Sam (he is not entirely "good," we are to see from his relationship with the much younger, pointedly named Rose Lamb from the Girls' Friendly House) hires Helmi to work in his restaurant. He is thus contrasted with the many middle-class Anglo-Canadian women who will not hire Helmi.

While the message is partly that these women ought to be ashamed of themselves for failing to do their duty in helping a new Canadian and a mother of the race, it is also embedded in contemporary debate about the so-called "White Woman's Labour Law" first enacted in Saskatchewan in 1912. As Constance Backhouse has pointed out, the legislation was originally called "An Act to Prevent the Employment of Female Labour in Certain Capacities." This "racially neutral phraseology" masked what she notes were its racially specific targets: "No person," the law held, "shall employ in any capacity any white woman or girl or permit any white woman or girl to reside in or lodge or to work in or, save as a *bona fide* customer in a public apartment thereof only, to frequent any restaurant, laundry or other place of business or amusement owned, kept or managed by any Japanese, Chinaman, or other Oriental person" (cited in Backhouse 1999, 136).

The law, as Sarah Carter has observed, had the effect of limiting women's ability to find employment. It thus did not so much protect

white women as force them to find more and more obscure ways
to earn an income (1997, 198). It is possible to see this circumstance
being played out in Helmi's story: When she takes the work, it is
seen by men to be detrimental to her reputation, but it does not
affect her virtue. Major Gowsett, the "bad" magistrate who does
not want to marry Jack and Helmi and who urges Jack to falsify
the union, writes to a friend: "'I saw the Finn girl again. She is in
a Chinese restaurant, working at night,' and he underlined the last
three words" (1925, 250). Major Gowsett's implications would be
readily understood by readers in the 1920s, who were certainly
familiar with the idea that, as Emily Murphy put it in *The Black
Candle*, white women were likely to be entrapped in Chinese "chop-
suey" houses and "noodle parlors" (cited in Backhouse 1999, 144).
Thus Colonel Blackwood, when Jack goes to see him to find Helmi,
reiterates the weighty information he has received: "This Milander
girl has gone back to her old associates, the Chinese. She is in one
of the all-night eating-houses. I suppose you know what it means
when a white girl goes into one of these places" (1925, 264).

Kay J. Anderson outlines "what it means" in her account of the
work of one Vancouver-based reformer to bring in legislation preventing white women from working in Chinese restaurants: "What
particularly concerned the retired colonel were the deeds he claimed
were being committed against young and inexperienced waitresses
who were 'induced ... to prostitute themselves with Chinese.' Foster
believed that contact would be set up inside restaurant booths and
that after working hours women would go to Chinese quarters,
'where immorality took place.' New staff members were very
quickly influenced to become 'loose.' It was also established, said
Foster, 'that the majority of Vancouver's known prostitutes had for-
merly been employed in Chinatown restaurants, thus indicating they
had started on their careers of vice through their early association
with those cafes'" (1995, 160).

Jack also knows what it means, as he had earlier understood the
implications when he was shown the newspaper story of Helmi's
arrest at the time they were being married. It is clear when Jack is
shown the account of Helmi's escape from the Girls' Friendly Home
that her arrest "in a Chinese den" situates her in an underworld of
sex as well as drugs, and conveys, as Davis and Hallett have suggested, "more than a hint of white slavery and prostitution" (1994,
249). Jack's response to the news is to anxiously reconsider Helmi's

sexual purity: "He couldn't – he wouldn't [believe that of Helmi].
There were no dark chapters in the boy's own life. He had lived
the clean, active life of a decent, funloving youth. He knew of the
evils in the world, having worked with gangs of men who spoke of
their carousals without shame, but he had always been repelled by
the coarseness, the vulgarity of it all. It couldn't be – Helmi was as
sweet and pure as a prairie flower" (1925, 166). Jack has faith then,
but, eventually, he too succumbs to the anxiety that circulates
around him; he leaves to go overseas, believing Helmi has "fallen."

McClung is certainly engaging with and drawing her readers'
attention to the question of white slavery that she had earlier
addressed in *In Times Like These*, as well as to the questions raised
by the White Woman's Labour Law. Helmi, when she gives birth,
is *like* a fallen woman. When she looks for work, she is *like* a girl
struggling to lift herself up. When she takes work in a Chinese
restaurant, she is *like* what readers would see as a woman familiar
with an underworld of sexual danger. However, while Helmi's narrative thus appears to reproduce a story of decline and sexual danger, it maintains the upward movement that is based on her virtue
and value – her "gold." The parallels are clear, but so too is the
argument being made in the book that the problem is not inherent
in the woman; rather, the problem is social and cultural. As is the
case for the representation of the women in *Purple Springs* who
must appear to be "immoral" if they are to maintain their virtue
and their economic self-sufficiency, the configuration of Helmi's
work in a Chinese restaurant is ambivalent.

McClung, who had been working as a member of the legislative
assembly in Alberta to raise the minimum wage for women and to
change laws that affected their ability to be self-sufficient (dower
law, married women's property law, divorce law), seems also to
have weighed in with the working women who were themselves, as
Carter has shown, opposing the White Woman's Labour Law and
with other feminists such as Helen Gregory McGill. As Backhouse
notes, McGill, one of Canada's first white female judges, held that
the "real issue ... was 'protection [of women] from exploitation,
moral or financial'" (1991, 144). McClung draws attention to this
kind of financial exploitation when she notes that Helmi worked
in Eagle Mines "all day long for twenty-five dollars a month, while
the poorest man in the mines had four dollars a day and only
worked eight hours" (1925, 139). Helmi does not suffer by her

work in the "better" Sam's restaurant (although she might, we are
to see, have been in danger in the first, "bad" Sam's Chop-Suey
House). What is highlighted then is not the danger of Sam's culture
but the failure of Anglo-Canadian society – and especially the middle-
class Anglo-Saxon women who were supposed by eugenists and
eugenic feminists to be the last real hope for the preservation of the
race – to protect her.

Painted Fires, like the Watson trilogy, is a eugenical romance. Its
happy ending is understood to mark the conclusion of a dysgenic
state and the beginning of a new social order with a maternal
woman at the front and centre of the community and the nation,
and her children growing up in a better world that she has been
instrumental in producing. What is implicit in the conclusion is that
this kind of community, where, as the playing children indicate, the
nation's future lies, is an ideal of assimilation, the result not of mere
happenstance but of virtue, determination, "honest toil" (1915,
158), and, most importantly, of women's work. Just as Pearl Watson
leads the community toward the eradication of the linked racial
poisons, alcohol and tuberculosis, and opens the way to the racially
revivifying Purple Springs, in *Painted Fires* Helmi has almost sin-
glehandedly brought this ideal site for the reproduction of the race
into existence.

The happy ending indicates that this novel, while focusing on the
pressing contemporary question of "open door" immigration, is
nonetheless, like all of McClung's fiction, ultimately about the
promise of the West for the renewal of the Anglo-Saxon race, the
hazards presented to that renewal by the lax morals and lawlessness
she saw as an effect of too much masculinity (1915, 147), and the
importance of women's work in the achievement of that promise.
Indeed, because it is an "immigration story," *Painted Fires* is actually about the preservation of "the race"; that is, it is concerned
with immigration as it was seen to affect the future of the empire
in the West. The story of Helmi's many "narrow escapes" is
intended to serve the didactic purpose of exposing the "truth"
about the kind of reception that newcomers might expect to receive
in Canada. Moreover, it was a warning to Anglo-Canadian settler
culture in the West that, if it failed to assimilate "foreigners" and,
especially, to recognize the reproductive value of "foreign" women
– at least, of those considered to be "assimilable" – it stood to

forfeit the racially regenerative function offered in the West, as immigrationist rhetoric suggested, quite possibly for the last time.

In her autobiography McClung wrote that in *Painted Fires* she "wanted to portray the struggles of a young girl who found herself in Canada dependent upon her own resources with everything to learn" (1945, 237). These struggles have less to do with the "false flattery" that McClung notes was propagated by immigrationists than with the sexual danger presented to the young white women who held the promise of the future of "the race" in their wombs as well as in their characters and their work. *Painted Fires* performs the work McClung saw herself doing, described by the Girls' Society leader, Miss Rodgers: "We are making a new country here in Canada, and we will love it best of all because we are making it. We are making paths and laying foundations, and that is what makes life here so interesting" (47). Helmi is a "stranger," but, as the novel reminds us repeatedly, she is a definitively white and assimilable one, McClung maintains, "worth the trouble."

PART FOUR

Eugenic Feminism and "Indian Work"

8

Re-Forming "Indianness"
The Eugenic Politics of Assimilation

One thing that has kept back missionary work is a silly, ignorant half-truth to which many people hold tenaciously, that is the comfortable theory that native races are holier, happier and better people generally before they are touched by Christianity. This half-truth calls for a pitiable confession; so called Christian nations are not entirely Christian, and have dealt terribly with pagan races. Civilization, which brought Christianity, has brought vices to the black and red man, but that is not the fault of Christianity. Christianity is a liberator. It sets the captive free from superstition and sin. Every foreign missionary will tell you that. And we know it is true in the case of our native Indians.

The belief that Indians were better off before the missionaries came has an appeal to people who like to have a good reason for not supporting missions. It gives a high-minded, even an ethical, flavour to the little streak of meanness which most of us have. But it will not stand investigation.

McClung, "Before They Call," 1937

In English Canada in the early years of the century, non-Anglo-Saxon immigration was regarded, as Woodsworth put it in his 1909 study and as *Painted Fires* suggests, as a "problem." It would be addressed through the processes of "Christianizing" and "Canadianizing," and through assimilation – at least for those categories that were seen to be assimilable into an imagined white national community. The categories of the unassimilable were, for Woodsworth, non-white peoples, amongst whom he included Africans, African-Americans, and "Orientals," as well as the indigenous First Nations peoples of North America, who were seen to pose a different kind of "problem" and to require a different kind of work in the development of Anglo-

imperial Canada. Understood as a benevolent enterprise of missionary "uplift," the work that reformers turned upon the putatively
unassimilable was definitively eugenic: its objective was the breeding
out of undesirable racial characteristics through the eradication of
the undesirable race. Racial "otherness" was, in other words, itself
constructed as a racial poison, its very presence a threat to white
dominance and the growth of the white dominion. This was certainly
one of the fundamental principles leading to the White Woman's
Labour Law in 1912 and to numerous other acts of racial protectionism in Canada, including, as Angus McLaren shows, the Alberta
Sexual Sterilization Bill.

For Canada's settler culture in the early years of the century, the
most pressing concern in the construction of the white dominion
was still referred to as the "Indian problem." The supposedly "vanishing race" had not disappeared, and eugenic nation-builders
sought to find a way to address the continued presence of the First
Nations. McClung would take up this "problem" in her writing,
both in the material she produced under the auspices of the Methodist and, subsequently, United Church home missions, and in her
fiction. McClung's rhetoric for the work of Methodist home missions is a crucial part of what Methodist missionary James Shaver
Woodsworth defined as "laying the foundations of empire in righ-
teousness and truth ... moulding the institutions of the future ...
shaping the destiny of the country" (1917, 11) by clearing the
"new" land, not only in the colonization and cultivation of the
western Canadian territory by white settlers but in emptying it of
aboriginal peoples, literally and symbolically.

In the first volume of her autobiography, *Clearing in the West*
(1935), McClung explains why her family, in expansionist transit
in 1880 from settled Ontario to the newly opened province of
Manitoba, decided not to remain in Winnipeg, by this time a bur-
geoning urban centre, but to move on and take up a new farm on
the Souris River, some five hundred miles north. "Let us go on,"
McClung quotes her mother, Letitia Mooney, as saying. "Let us go
to an all-white settlement. There are too many jet black eyes and
high cheekbones here. I like them very well when they belong to
the neighbours' children, but I would not like them in my grand-
children. We came here, John, for the children's sake, not ours, and
we'll do our best for them every way" (52). McClung immediately
disowns her mother's sentiments, but in such a way as to render

ambiguous her own position on the question of interracial reproduction. "I couldn't see why she objected," she writes of her
response as a child of seven (52). As the little anecdote she subsequently tells of "Indian Tommy" and his "roaring drunk" mother
shows, however, she may well "see" as an adult writing in 1935
why an "all-white settlement" would have been preferable for Letitia
Mooney, whose thoughts were all of the future of her own children
and of the promise of the West as a part of the British Empire.

Although she represents her mother's view of "Indian Tommy"
with a consciousness that it is problematic, McClung also points
out that her mother was, "above all things, loyal to her own. Her
family, her relatives, her country ... Great Britain was the greatest
and most God-fearing country in the world, and Queen Victoria
was the hand-maiden of the Lord" (173). In Letitia Mooney's view,
as McClung indicates, the racial preservation provided by an "all-
white settlement" serves as an index of the loyalty of imperial pio-
neers such as the Mooneys are shown to be in *Clearing in the West*.
Indeed, like the Watson family, the Mooneys are suggestively presented as "the real Empire builders" (1921, 71), the really loyal
imperialists, committed to hewing out a new space for Anglo-
Saxondom. When McClung positions herself within this framework,
she tacitly endorses her mother's imperialist rhetoric.

Settlers like the Mooneys moving westward in the 1870s and '80s
were predisposed to regard themselves as empire-builders by pro-
British immigrationist propaganda that glorified then, as it would
into the 1920s, the last best West as not only uncultivated but also,
increasingly, unpopulated. McClung, like many others, seems to have
put a willing faith in the notion that the First Nations of the western
provinces were, along with their counterparts in the East, approach-
ing racial extinction, the "vanishing races singing their death-song as
they are swept on to the cataract of oblivion," as W.D. Lighthall
suggested in *Songs of the Great Dominion* in 1889 (xxi).

In *Clearing in the West* there is little to suggest that McClung
saw white English-Canadian settlers as displacing First Nations peoples or that the white settlers did not bring significantly compensa-
tory advantages as they swept into the North West. In fact, not
surprisingly at a time that English-Canadians were congratulating
themselves for what was represented as their more humane treatment of western aboriginal peoples than they had seen earlier in
the United States, McClung blames American buffalo hunters for

having wiped out the herds and forcing the Indians northward, leaving the territory empty for settlers like the Mooneys (1935, 84). Dispossession, in other words, was represented as having *preceded* expansion, and not having occurred as a direct result of Anglo-Saxon settlement. Already "vanishing," the aboriginal "races" were not to be seen as having been forced out by expansion; rather, the white settlers were to be recognized as simply moving into a vacated territory that could be seen as still untouched because it had not been extensively farmed or industrialized.

This view, as Leslie Monkman observes, persisted until well into the twentieth century: "As late as 1941, Stephen Leacock was writing that after the voyage of the Vikings, 'the continent remained, as it had been for uncounted centuries, empty. We think of prehistoric North America as inhabited by the Indians, and have based on this a sort of recognition of ownership on their part. But this attitude is hardly warranted. The Indians were too few to count. Their use of the resources of the continent was scarcely more than that by crows and wolves, their development of it nothing'" (Leacock cited in Monkman, 1981, 7).

In 1935, with a similarly imperialist inflection, McClung was writing that the "few" Indians she encountered as the Mooneys travelled north in Manitoba were themselves "hardly warranted" in counting their own losses, territorial or otherwise. "At Portage la Prairie," she writes of their journey to the Souris River in 1880, "we stopped at the Hudson's Bay store and bought further supplies ... Indians in their blankets stood at the door of the store, not saying a word to anyone, and from their masklike faces no one could tell their thoughts. No doubt they resented the influx of white settlers and the carts loaded with fur, passing on their way to Winnipeg. But the buffalo was gone, their best friend, source of food and clothes, so perhaps the struggle was over, now that the battle was lost. I hoped they did not mind" (1935, 68).

There is an undertone of concern – or guilt – about the displacement of First Nations peoples here as elsewhere in this first volume of the autobiography. McClung's hope that "they did not mind" the "influx of white settlers" and the loss of the land does not, however, as Doug Owram has pointed out of expansionist perception, indicate any sense that it was not eminently right and desirable for white settlers to move westward: "In the expansionist mind, sympathy [for the dispossessed aboriginal] in no way contradicted the right of European civilization to supplant the native. The certainty that their own civilization was superior and the ubiquitous doctrine of progress made them accept without question the idea that it was 'necessary that the Indian hunting-ground should in large measure be given up to the plough and the sickle of the white man'" (132).[1]

Any continued concern for the situation of the dispossessed aboriginal was resolved "in the contemporary mind," Owram suggests, by the argument that "while the displacement of the native was necessary and perhaps inevitable, there was nevertheless a duty on the part of the new civilization to aid the Indian ... With the Indian as the ward of the state, steps could be taken to protect him from the harmful effects of white culture while teaching him its benefits ... Eventually the settlement of the West would uplift the native from his state as 'a member of a barbarous, heathen horde, wandering aimlessly over this vast continent' and make him instead 'an enfranchised citizen of the first Christian nation in the world'" (132).

The civilizing mission of the British Empire thus purported to "provide the Indian with far more than he had lost" (132): "the Indian" would "not mind" the influx of white settlers once taught "the benefits" of white culture. McClung notes her sister Hannah's having put it thus: "The country belonged to the Indians and half-breeds ... We must not forget that. I know they have made little use of it and must yield it to white settlers in time, but there's enough territory for everyone if it is handled right, and they could be easily appeased and satisfied" (169). What is at stake is not the right of First Nations peoples to occupy the territory, to which they are seen here to have "yielded" ownership on the basis of their perceived failure to cultivate it, but the correct "handling" of them. Progress, we are to see, is inevitable and justified, but the processes of civilization are to be tempered with mercy. The "Indians," like children, will be "easily appeased."

When McClung recounts in the first volume of her autobiography her family's move from Ontario to Manitoba in 1880, she does not describe any fear of retaliation, but she does relate an anecdote that conveys – primarily (as in the account of Hannah's speech) in order to undermine – the sense of any lasting injustice done the indigenous people of Canada through imperial expansion. Stranded in an isolated settlement in the family's first winter in the west, Hannah becomes ill, and none of Letitia Mooney's remedies has any effect on the child. When Letitia's fear turns to despair, she articulates a kind of collective and deeply repressed cultural guilt, crying, "My little girl is dying for want of a doctor, in this cursed place – that never should have been taken from the Indians ... The Indians have their revenge on me now, for it's tearing my heart out, to see my little girl die before my eyes" (79).

What makes the event significant for McClung is the appearance of the new Methodist minister from the nearby settlement of Millford at precisely the crucial moment both for Hannah's life and for Letitia's faith in the empire. He brings medicine in his bag, and, even more importantly, faith of the kind that Tennyson defined in his famous epilogue to the 1873 edition of *Idylls of the King*, as "the tone of empire[,] the faith/ That made us rulers" ("To the Queen," 18–19). For McClung, the appearance of this man is nothing less than a sign from God and the foundation, she later avers, of her lifelong belief in the importance of home missions ("Before They Call," 1937, 5–6). What is also implicit in this little narrative is the way the minister/missionary disempowers the malevolent and vindictive natives that Letitia has introduced as bogeys, and returns lifesaving and civilizing authority to the imperialists. With the return of health, significantly, comes the restoration of moral stability to the Mooney household. Such, at any rate, are the values with which McClung imbues the story when she tells it in 1935.

After this affirmation of the propriety and authority of white settlers, McClung describes her mother's own subsequent ministrations among the natives they encounter in the West.[2] Letitia Mooney, whose desire to preserve an all-white racial purity is betrayed by her comments about the dangers of mixing British blood with aboriginal, is later painted as something of a missionary herself, offering assistance and instruction in personal hygiene and health, the necessary correlatives of moral reform for McClung as for most reformers in "the age of light, soap, and water" (Valverde 1991). In these acts, Letitia's sense of superiority is as evident as her good intentions. She is committed to educating the local native women in what would later be called mothercraft, and the story of Letitia's treatment of a sick baby is a significant forerunner of McClung's representation in 1937 of the importance of home missions among First Nations peoples, as well as of her own feminist work to create in Canada "an enlightened culture of motherhood." That is, ministering to a sick baby in the 1880s, Letitia produces a marked conversion in the impassive or "indifferent" mother, as well as "curing" the child. When she hands back the baby after applying goose grease to his chest, the mother's face, we are told, "lost its mask of indifference. She actually smiled as she took the baby in her arms" (1935, 189). With this smile the woman not only seems to *forgive* the white settlers, she "actually" indicates that she has seen that they have brought good things to the West. This, for McClung, is the civilizing mission of the empire at its smallest but most representative level.

McClung returned to the story of the Methodist minister in a 1937 pamphlet, produced under the auspices of the Board of Home Missions for what was by then the United Church of Canada. This pamphlet reprises many of the concerns addressed in an earlier pamphlet for the Methodist Woman's Missionary Society (MWMS), even echoing its title: the first (undated) document is entitled "An Insistent Call," the 1937 one "Before They Call."[3] McClung begins this second home missions pamphlet with an abbreviated version of the story of the missionary who saved the Mooney family's first winter in Manitoba in 1880 (5–6). "That was my first contact with the Board of Home Missions," she writes. "It did much to convince me that there is life in the Church" (6). Although McClung's rhetoric in 1937, when the expansion of the empire was no longer a pressing concern, tends to configure the imperialist sentiment underlying the story in nostalgic terms, as it also does in *Clearing in the West*, her "call" for home missions is no less insistent than it was in her first home missions "call," a preface to the Winnipeg All People's Mission annual report in 1911–12 ("Organized Helpfulness"), the MWMS pamphlet, or her 1921 plea to British Methodists at the Fifth Ecumenical Methodist Conference in London, England, to recognize the need in Canada for support for home missions.[4] Indeed, in this 1937 pamphlet McClung articulates with a precision and clarity not perceptible in her earlier work an imperialist view of the *necessity* of assimilating aboriginal peoples: she positions First Nations missionary activity as the first concern of the home missions, before "foreign work at home," and her "call" is to the "sound, kind, courageous and sympathetic" "heart of humanity" to respond to the "need" that she describes in Canada.

McClung's return to the scene of expansion in the autobiographical *Clearing in the West* is thus not merely evidence of expansionist perception revisited and defended. Rather, the case she makes for the benefits of white culture for aboriginal Canadians must also be situated within the half-century of missionary rhetoric she produced under the auspices of the Methodist and, subsequently, the United Church Board of Home Missions, and within her continued concern about the work of assimilation in the 1930s. "The Indians in Canada," she maintains, "are not decreasing as some people think they are. The work of the Indian schools, in which the Church and the Government combine their efforts to fit the boys and girls for life, goes on successfully, and to-day there are efficient Indian farmers, teachers, engineers and ministers to bear witness to the success of this branch of missionary work" (1937, 11). Her point in this United Church Mission Services pamphlet is that it is the "duty" of Christian Canadians in 1937, as Woodsworth argued it was in 1909, to uplift "our Indian," separate "him" from his community and his cultural identity, and integrate him into Saxondom (Woodsworth 1909, 159–60). This, for Woodsworth, and, indeed, for his father, James, the superintendent of North-West Missions of the Methodist Church from 1887 to 1915, is what imperialism "should mean."

"As a part of the British Empire," Woodsworth senior would argue in 1917 in his memoir of *Thirty Years in the Canadian North-West*, "Canada must share in the responsibilities of the Empire on whose dominions the sun never sets. To her sons, Imperialism should mean more than the consolidation of her several units into a national whole. Imperialism should mean the improvement of the greatest opportunity the world has ever presented for the application of those principles which alone can truly exalt any people and cause God's glory to dwell in the land" (xv).

"Indian work," as James Woodsworth defined it in 1917, was to be regarded as the most important of "the responsibilities of the Empire" and, moreover, "the most honorable work of the whole Christian ministry – the original creative work of going where no man had gone of which Paul had boasted" (6). This statement of what imperialism "should mean" articulated an extremely popular view of the civilizing mission of the empire in English Canada, particularly as it was conceived after Confederation in 1867, when Canada was still politically and emotionally bound to England while formed as a dominion with its own government. Woodsworth suggests here that expansionism and colonization are motivated not by economic interest but by a heartfelt desire to share Anglo-Saxon moral enlightenment, technology, and cultural literacy with constituencies still regarded as being lower on an evolutionary scale than the putatively "Northern" peoples. These are what Agnes Maule Machar configured as "a little cluster of Northern Lights shining amid the Northern darkness" (1893, 191), a "darkness of savagery and heathenism" (373) in her children's book, *Marjorie's Canadian Winter*, which deliberately situates late nineteenth-century Christian reform within a history of missionary activity in Canada.[5]

Both Woodsworths were imperialists first, their rhetoric of Christian social reform the result of at least three decades of imperial social reform, a movement whose discourse dominates social and political thought in English Canada as much as Bernard Semmel points out that it does in Britain after the mid-1880s. J.S. Woodsworth was the head of the All People's Mission in Winnipeg, an organizer, with Tommy Douglas, of the Co-operative Commonwealth Federation, the author of two studies of immigration in Canada, *Strangers within Our Gates, or Coming Canadians* (1909) and *My Neighbour* (1911), as well as of a series of articles promoting the sexual sterilization of "mental defectives" in Canada.[6] His Christian social reform work, in conjunction with his left-leaning politics, demonstrates perhaps even more vividly than does McClung (who was politically identified with the Liberal party and threw her ideological support behind the more conservative United Farmers Association) what Semmel calls "the strange union of socialism and imperialism" characterizing Anglo-Saxon social reform in the late nineteenth and early twentieth centuries (9). This "strange union" presents itself most dramatically in Woodsworth's articulations of the Indian "problem" and how it ought to be resolved through the good works of the Methodist home missions. Both Woodsworth and McClung held that the "solution" to the "Indian problem" was missionary.

In *Strangers within Our Gates*, Woodsworth classifies "the Indians" as the least desirable of all the non-British "strangers" he discusses, and cites the comments of a fellow missionary, the Rev. Thompson Ferrier, on the "main hope" of Indian education.[7] "As fast as our Indian, whether of mixed or full blood, is capable of taking care of himself," writes Ferrier, "it is our duty to set him on his feet, and sever forever the ties that bind him either to his tribe or the Government. Both Church and State should have, as a final goal, the destruction and end of treaty and reservation life" (cited in Woodsworth 1909, 159–60). Woodsworth supplements Ferrier's comments with the observation that, although much "missionary work, evangelistic, educational, industrial and medical," had been done among First Nations peoples, more was urgently required: "Many are devout Christians living exemplary lives, but there are still 10,202 Indians in our Dominion, as grossly pagan as were their ancestors, or still more wretched, half civilized, only to be debauched. Surely the Indians have a great claim upon Canadian Christians!" (160).

Contrary to what Leacock suggested in 1941, people *were* counting "the Indians" in Canada, and Woodsworth's numbers indicate that, in fact, a close count was being kept in the interests of monitoring the presence of the First Nations. What is implicit in Woodsworth's enumeration is the effect of a countdown: "still 10,202 Indians" *to go* before this home mission is accomplished. Twenty years later McClung would point out to her readers that the numbers were still not decreasing, while the ranks were clearly becoming depleted of those still interested in the kind of Christian imperial-social reform she and Woodsworth supported. Thus she was reissuing the call she had made earlier on behalf of Woodsworth's All People's Mission in Winnipeg and for the Methodist Woman's Missionary Society, and reminding her readers of the need to keep up the good work of empire. Interest and volunteer support for home missions, however, as for other "organized helpfulness" of the kind that burgeoned in women's organizations at the end of the nineteenth century and into the 1920s, had clearly waned by the time of the Depression.

In the 1937 pamphlet McClung illustrates her point about the "meanness" and "ignoran[ce]" of "people who like to have a good reason for not supporting missions" with a story that is configured, like the appearance of the missionary in 1880, as "A Miracle." As in the earlier story, moral and physical, personal and imperial health are rendered as interdependent; "rescue" comes when First Nations people are saved through mission work from their "superstitions" and brought from darkness into the light of Christian salvation, as well as, of course, soap and water. To be thus enlightened and scrubbed of inherent "darkness" is literally in this story to be *re-formed*, not only offered salvation for the soul but remade into a new identity that is no longer aboriginal, here not only morally obscure but spiritually *deformed*. The "case" McClung recounts is the story of "little Emily, the Indian child, who was, according to the old tradition, cursed with an evil spirit" (9). That is, she "was deformed by the dislocation of both hips, and the only thing her mother could do for her was to beat her poor little emaciated body to drive out the evil spirits ... Emily's deformed little body was black and blue from blows and her life was a hell of fear and pain" (9). Emily is rescued from these obviously dreadful – and implicitly "savage" – circumstances by a missionary. "He saw this pitiful child," writes McClung, "... and his heart was moved with compassion ... He asked Emily's parents if he could have her, and they were quite willing. Emily was no asset, and I believe it grieved them to have to beat her, so it would suit them well to be rid of her" (9). The suggestion that Emily's parents are both "savage" and subnormal is implicit in the alacrity with which they give up their child: in this narrative, they are as infantilized as is "little Emily," and, indeed, it is *their* moral deformity that we are to see in Emily's "little body."

The church is thus empowered to have the child and to raise her in an environment that will eradicate the effects of the past and convert her into a useful citizen who is not an Indian. In this act of forcible assimilation, reform, and symbolic disinfection of the "savagery" in Emily, the church is assisted by education, medicine, and soap and water in a process of Christian "healing" (10): Emily is to be *cured* of her "Indianness" along with her deformity. Once she has been "washed ... and brought to the Indian School at Brandon," "wonderful things" begin to happen for her (9). "There have been operations, and long periods in hospitals. Now Emily can walk as well as anyone. She goes to school. She has been taught to laugh and play, make her own clothes, and live like other children" (9). McClung concludes without irony, "Emily is a distinct personality now" – now, that is, that she has been taught to be "like other children." Little Emily, in this anecdote, does not simply represent the abused children of ignoble "savages" in the Canadian West: she is a figure for all First Nations people who will follow the lighted missionary path and find civilization and religion, reconstituted, in effect, in the image of white civilization. Not only actual children such as Emily but, we are told, all "our Indians receive the message with a childlike simplicity" (10).[8] For this reason, McClung's "call" to missionaries to carry "the message" is as "insistent" as it was in her earlier writings.

In 1945, McClung recounts how her own perception of one First Nations man was changed only when she learned that he had a son overseas in the war. "Then," she writes, "suddenly it occurred to ... us that the running board of a car was not the place where this man should be riding. We stopped the car, and we found room for him in the back seat by putting one big valise on the front. He was no longer a plain Indian with torn clothes and a dirty face. He was one of us – and one who had made a big contribution. We were all citizens of the British Empire; we were all of the great family of the Next-of-Kin, and, after all, what is a dirty face and a torn coat?" (158).⁹

It is a telling moment "of illumination," as McClung calls it, characterized in terms of the salutary effects of missionary work upon the production of useful imperial citizens. McClung blesses the mission for having produced such a man, with such a son, implying that this is the most desirable result of Christian and imperial attention to First Nations Canadians. The re-formed Indian, like the re-formed European immigrant of *Painted Fires* and the re-formed drinker of *The Second Chance* and *When Christmas Crossed "The Peace,"* joins the purity army McClung saw fighting to protect a "race" whose purpose she saw as "life and growth."

9

"Called to [the] Mission"

Interpellating First Nations and Métis Mothers in "Red and White" and "Babette"

And now, after twenty-five years [of government reserve policy] – what of the women? The visitor to the Canadian west sees bright-eyed, chubby, happy-looking damsels; though it must be admitted the matrons are still haggard and worn. The Industrial Schools, which have been established for the training of young Indians, and the efforts of the missionaries have had their effects.
  Henriette Forget, "The Indian Women of the Western Provinces," 1900

Although "Indian work" represents a significant part of McClung's race-based and eugenic feminist reform work in a half century of writing for the Methodist and the United Church Mission Services, she published only two stories that focus upon the "Indian problem," as she and Woodsworth defined it in their home missions rhetoric. "Babette" appeared in 1907 in *Canada West*, a journal initially produced in London, Ontario, and a forum for pro-British immigrationist rhetoric. The second story, "Red and White," was published in serial form from November 1921 to February 1922 in the *Western Home Monthly*, a settler periodical produced in Winnipeg. Both stories focus on First Nations people who have already been "re-formed," in both cases through residential or mission schools. Both stories foreground the problematic of McClung's feminism and her fiction as a eugenical undertaking. Both have been republished in *Stories Subversive*, the 1999 selection of short stories edited by Marilyn I. Davis.

"Babette" was written while McClung was in Winnipeg, at a time when she was involved with the work of Woodsworth's All People's Mission. It is a story that reinforces the distinctions between constructed categories of race in much the way the later story "Red and White" also does. Both works are stories of expansionism, and of feminism at work in the last best West. Babette and Minnie, the heroines of the two stories, both perform the kind of socially hygienic work of the McClungian maternal feminist: they clean up and improve their society, beginning with those nearest at hand.

But "Babette" is not *about* Babette at all, except in so far as it demonstrates the imagined effects of residential schooling upon a Métis child. It is actually about George Shaw, the colonizing Englishman who needs some feminine intervention. We see at the beginning of the story that he has significantly lapsed from Christianity: "If George Shaw had been a Christian Scientist on the morning of the twentieth of October, he would have said that he had too much mortal mind. But he was a Methodist, and one who had departed from his first love, so he merely said that he felt like the very devil" (1907, 49). His house is an index of his condition: "Ashes littered the floor. A sooty pot with a few black potatoes, boiled yesterday in their skins, stood on the back covers. Dirty dishes littered the table" (49).

When Henri, "the half-breed boy," arrives with Shaw's weekly supply of bread, his cleanliness is introduced as something that is not only a new phenomenon for him but one that serves primarily to highlight the squalor of Shaw's cabin. Henri's "recent and mighty conflict with soap and water" is noted as the work of his sister, Babette, freshly returned from the mission school in Winnipeg. "Babette is wan beeg swell," notes Henri. "Babette clean her teet' wan, two, t'ree tam every day. She wash her ear. She sweep, scrub, clean all tam. Mais oui, you should but see Babette. She is good peopl'" (50). She is also newly critical of Shaw: "'Babette say you leev lak wan dog,'" remarks Henri, "watching Shaw furtively" (50). Babette is thus *like* Pearl and Helmi – now. Earlier, we learn, she was like Henri, but has managed to transcend what is implicitly represented as her racial and cultural disposition towards uncleanliness.

Henri plants the seed in Shaw's mind that Babette is setting her cap for him, something that is entirely ludicrous and also disturbing for the Englishman. Henri also suggests that there is a discrepancy between Shaw's house and his skin colour, a discrepancy that obtains with precisely the opposite effect for Henri and Babette. That is, Shaw does not live "like white folks"; that Babette and now Henri do is an indication of some kind of fundamental reversal. They, we are to see, might be expected to be dirty; white-skinned Shaw is expected to be clean. Henri's visit leads him to perceive the nature of the problem as it is to be understood as inherent in racialized standards and behaviour. At the end of the autumn day, Shaw becomes conscious of contrast between the "dismal little shanty with its dirt and cheerlessness" and "his English home." He admits that, "yes, Babette was right, he did live like a dog" (50–2). When he sees that Babette has come in during the day and cleaned his house and prepared his dinner, his first thought is to return to Henri's suggestion that she would be a good wife. He locks the door, in a gesture of literally attempting to keep the danger of racial mixing out of the imperial domestic microcosm.

At one level Babette represents a set of "instinctive" feminine characteristics that McClung saw linking all women across racial and cultural boundaries.[10] These essential elements erupt in such "feminine" desires as housecleaning and childcare, much more important to McClung as a sign of "true" womanhood than the simple biological desire to have children. Training, of almost any kind, would enable women, in McClung's view, to exploit these instincts for the common good: to clean, to cook, to nurse, to teach, to care for society as for one's own children. Babette, after she returns from the residential school in Winnipeg where she has learned how to put natural feminine desires into practice, begins to do what McClung enjoins all "mother-women" to do throughout her writing: she puts her skills to work to clean up more of the world than her own small corner – what McClung always argues is the primary concern of feminism. Babette begins with her own body, then extends these learned skills to purify her own home and her family, and, before the end of the story, moves in on the Englishman's house.

Like the condition of her own home before her return from Winnipeg, the squalor and filth of the Englishman's home is both an index of and the metaphorical figure for his moral condition. He needs, we are to see, to clean up his whole attitude, to behave like a proper Englishman in the colonies: working on the frontier to expand the British Empire, acting simultaneously as pioneer and missionary, forging a new site for the fostering and development of Anglo-Saxondom in the West. Babette leaves a note on his table:

Dear Mister Pshaw! No I don't want you. Thank you all the same. I cleaned up your shantey to let you see how it feals to live like white folks. I have a gentleman frend in Winnipeg he wears clene collars and can alwas find his combe no more at present.
    Babette Morin. (52)

Good men – and good imperialists – are discernible in their personal hygiene, itself an index of social hygiene. The white pioneer men whom McClung represents in so many of her stories must practise cleanliness if there is to be advance and progress of the empire: in McClung's narratives of settlement, these men *always* need women, "finger-posts on the way to right living," to help them.

Implicit in both "Babette" and "Red and White" is the notion that the best "Indian work" is done by indigenous women with white blood (both Babette and Minnie Hardcastle are of mixed ancestry) who have learned putatively "white" values, such as cleanliness, Christianity, sobriety, and sexual restraint. "Uplifted" to the point where they are able to extend their feminine house-cleaning and maternal caregiving instincts to their homes and communities, they are also noticeably *not* "uppity." Babette does not want to marry George Shaw not because he is slovenly – she knows she would be able to keep him tidy, for she has learned to do so at school in Winnipeg – but because she has a clear sense of boundaries. She participates in the maintenance of the imperial West *for* white settlers. Minnie makes a similar gesture at the end of "Red and White," commanding Johnny to quit his job and take up his own heritage. The story ends with Minnie announcing that she and Johnny Starblanket are going to go "down North" where his brothers are, and that they are going to take his mother, Rosie, as well. "There are too many people here," she says, "too much noise and crowds all the time, and never any quiet time any more. It's a right place for white people, but no good for Indians" (175). Like Babette, she has reinforced separation and has thus promoted the "civilizing mission."

If "Babette" is predicated on an ironic inversion of missionary work as a salient reminder to white settlers to behave "like white folks," "Red and White" is predicated on its readers understanding

that, like Kipling's East and West, the two racial categories indicated
in the title must remain separate in the assimiliationist culture of
the "new" country. Davis and Hallett have suggested that "As a
nonassimilationist tale 'Red and White' is well in advance of its
time. The sense that the Indian has a culture that he wants to preserve and survive in, and has a right to, is truly remarkable for the
1920s" (1994, 265). Fiamengo has noted that the story is "racist
in its certainty that all of its main character's traits, good and bad,
can be explained through his Indianness" (1999–2000, 79), but has
maintained that it also undertakes a powerful "analysis of the sys-
temic oppression of Native peoples – particularly white destruction
of their land and way of life" (79). The representation, however, of
"Red and White" as a "nonassimilationist tale" or even as a critique
of "white destruction" implies that the story is also written with
some desire "to preserve" Indian culture. In fact, "Red and White"
is best understood in conjunction with the home missionary position articulated by McClung in her Methodist and United Church
pamphlets and with the nativist and imperialist rhetoric of contemporaries such as Woodsworth. As such, its main concern is with the
"unassimilable" nature of aboriginal peoples and how that "problem" might best be addressed. The story's concluding line describes
Rosie and Johnny Starblanket and the "half-breed" Minnie Hardcastle as "three happy Indians about to enter into their native heritage of open air and sky" (1921–22, 175). This conclusion has a
vaguely morbid undercurrent, presenting without irony these three
"happy Indians" who are "thinking of the big country 'down north'
beckoning to them with its promise of peace and plenty and good
hunting" (175). Here, it is suggested, it will be possible to find a
"new" life that replicates the life of Johnny's "father and his grandfather and the older brothers who had fled before civilization's
choking breath" (136).

Despite the narrative's seeming condemnation of the encroachment
of "civilization" upon "the life to which all Indians belonged"
(136), the position in this story is not far from McClung's 1937
cry, "Tell Emily that she was better off under the old regime!"
(1907, 10). For instance, Rosie Starblanket, who "knew well the
ways of cleaning a house" (1921–22, 138) in part because she is
female ("the instinct to house-clean is inherent in women" [137]),
has also, like Babette, learned how to utilize this "instinct" from
white women: "Though she would not have admitted it, the cottage

dwellers had taught her many things; and if her heart had been heavier since their coming, her house at any rate had been cleaner. Curtains had appeared at the small windows, and vegetable dishes had mysteriously supplemented the functions of the black pot in which her potatoes and cabbages were boiled. Better methods of washing, too, had superseded the fire on the shore and the rubbing of clothes by hand on a stone" (138).

"Red and White" is "non-assimilationist" only because it takes the position with J.S. Woodsworth that "Indianness" is not assimilable. As a social purity text, its seeming focus on the problem of alcohol is a bit misleading. This is not a temperance tale *per se*, but one that addresses the ways that racial categories can seep into one another, and the ways that alcohol can facilitate that seepage, in much the same way that, according to Emily Murphy in *The Black Candle*, opium can lead white women to forget their duty to maintain racially separate categories. (Murphy published what were to be alarming photographs of white women lying with men of colour.) Alcohol, in McClung's fiction, is similarly a racial poison for whites, not only because of the effects it has on white bodies and their progeny but because of this kind of sexual danger. Alcohol, we see in the Watson trilogy, is the "bed" of tuberculosis; it is also, we see in "Red and White," potentially the "bed" of miscegenation. It is thus hazardous, in McClung's "Indian" stories, to the preservation of whiteness, so much "harder to keep clean," as Maggie observed in *Painted Fires* (1925, 19). "Indianness," within this framework of imperial and racial purity, itself becomes a racial poison.

The point of McClung's narrative, however, is not to promote an anti-assimilationist position but to suggest that temperance is not enough to ensure the peaceful existence of First Nations peoples in the Canadian West. Where the white settlers of *When Christmas Crossed "The Peace"* need only to have the disease of alcohol exorcised from their community in order for health, hygiene, and Christian principles to be reaffirmed, drink is only a part of the problem for the Starblankets and Minnie Hardcastle. That this problem is being presented as specifically racial in its origin is evident in the narrative's juxtaposition of the temperance question and John Starblanket's "primitive savage instincts" (1921–22, 158). "The law," McClung suggests, can only do so much to "civilize" aboriginals, for even the best "training and education" will "[break] down temporarily" (158) under certain conditions. Even before he has had a drink, "the glamor of the lights and the music" at the dance which is at the centre of the story's crisis produce an "exaltation" in Johnny that erases the effects of his schooling and result in "all the primitive savage instincts ... surging within him" (157–8): "He wanted action, noise, motion, excitement, admiration. If it had been forty years earlier he could have painted his face, sharpened his toma-hawk, and found an outlet for his turbulent soul in stalking some of the young braves of another tribe. But this was in the year of grace nineteen fourteen, and there were laws and conventions to be considered" (158).

Johnny has been only superficially "whitened" by his education and by temperance; there is a core of unassimilable "savagery" which no law can remedy: "To all intents John Starblanket was a white man, an employee of a great Railway, a young man of prom-ise, who held a position of trust. The law had placed a ban on the evil thing that had the power to set aside his training and turn him back to savagery again. But even the law cannot control that elu-sive, uncertain and variable factor which enters into every human equation. Individuals can find a way to evade and elude the law, and so make its good purposes to no effect. The law had tried to save John Starblanket from his enemy, but the law had failed" (158). The law, we are to understand, however, had not failed because of any inherent weakness on its part. The conflict between "red" and "white" that dominates the story is thus refigured as an "Indian" problem: the "white" side, here represented by the law, has held up its side, educating the native boy, giving him a "white man's" job and placing a "ban on the evil thing that had the power to ... turn him back to savagery again" (158). It is "the Indian" who has failed. The "enemies" of the story are not, after all, "Red and White," but all "red." The real battles are not, therefore, between the First Nations and the white settlers but are refigured as the genetic inevitability of "primitive" instincts. Johnny's enemy is not just drink but drink as it awakens the slumbering savage thinly disguised by a veneer of civilization. Prohibition, therefore, cannot save Johnny: his only recourse, we are shown, is to move away from temptation and to live with other natives.

Not only drink, in fact, but any "exaltation" or powerful emotion can cause the "training and education" of aboriginal people to "break down," the story suggests. Thus at moments of stress, both Johnny and Minnie revert to a broken English described as "the

Indian manner of speech." Minnie, whose father was white (130) and who looks white (Johnny describes her to his mother as "pure Indian in everything but looks" [131]), is, as Rosie fears, also "white" in her behaviour. Within the limits of the narrative, this means that she speaks well, works hard, and shows a concern with hygiene. Nonetheless, the "pure Indian" that Johnny perceives in Minnie emerges when she sees him holding the "white girl's bare elbow, and [bending] over her caressingly" (162). At this moment, "it was well for little Miss Speers that Minnie had no instrument of death in her hand, for Minnie's mind held but one thought. She was pure Indian now, with no restraint or compunction, and would have killed the girl as joyously as her grandfather had killed the bear at the falls where the rainbow throws its radiance" (162).

L.M. Montgomery configures a similarly essentialized and thinly disguised "savagery" in her story, "Tannis of the Flats," included in *Further Chronicles of Avonlea* (1920). Tannis, a Métis woman, discovering that the white man whom she loves has shifted his affections to a white woman, turns on him in fury. "Poor Tannis!" muses Jerome Carey, after she has "stalked away to her canoe." "How handsome she had looked in her fury – and how much like a squaw! The racial marks always come out plainly under the stress of emotion" (194). What he has failed to see, we are told, is that she is not *actually* civilized. Like Johnny Starblanket and Minnie Hardcastle, Tannis has a "very thin, but very deceptive, veneer of culture and civilization overlying the primitive passions and ideas of her nature" (Montgomery 1920, 189).

Such "primitive passions" likewise emerge when Minnie is addressing the magistrate Brown, brother of the eastern member of parliament who insults her in the hotel dining room and who illegally, under the early twentieth-century Canadian system of policing and "protecting" First Nations peoples, gives Johnny alcohol. When the magistrate self-righteously invokes the "law and order" his brother has been shown to have deliberately disrupted, Minnie, lapsing "into the Indian manner of speech," says, "he is good boy – never drinks – saving his money – nice – but white man takes him up to his room and gives him drink out of bottle – then white girl gets him at dance – coaxes him away into City here. He's good boy if damn whites only leave him alone" (1921–22, 171). What is telling here is not only Minnie's "Indian" diction but her obvious acceptance of the white perception of the infantilized Indian.

Johnny is helpless once he is set upon by the whites offering the drink he is forbidden by law and the racially mixed sexual union frowned upon by everyone in the story. For Johnny, as, implicitly for Minnie's mother, seduction by whites is irresistible; these two are not to be blamed for falling prey to the immoral characters Minnie describes as "damn whites." Thus Miss Speers's more serious and well-intentioned friend, Miss Brown – whose name parallels that of the "bad" magistrate Brown in what is a familiar strategy in those of McClung's narratives which purport to represent "good" and "bad" racial characteristics – admonishes Speers to "Leave the Indian boy alone – I'll bet he's got a girl some place. Have a heart, woman, and don't cut in on the native race. There ought to be a law against it, the same as selling liquor to them" (149). Seduction by whites, in other words, *is* "the same as selling liquor to them": in neither case will "the Indian" be able to resist. The responsibility, moreover, for controlling sex and liquor through "law and order" rests with the whites in the story: it is their duty not only to attempt to contain aboriginal "primitive instincts" but to counter the demoralizing influence of intemperate and immoral whites who would undo the work done for civilization by other whites, such as that done by the good mission teacher, Miss Bowden, who, it is suggested, is behind much of the "training and education" that have enabled both Johnny and Minnie to have "white" jobs.

As is the case for Minnie and for Montgomery's Tannis, the "pure Indian" in Johnny erupts when he is emotionally overwrought. Johnny, when he speaks to Minnie alone, uses the same kind of slangy patois that McClung identifies with so many of her urban characters. "Come on, Minnie," he says to her, "it's dandy out. Can't you get a spell off? You've often let the other girls out before it was all over. As long as you slave away they'll let you, girl – take that from me" (146). However, just a few minutes earlier, Johnny had taken on the "portly gentleman" who insulted Minnie in the dining room, and who, it is suggested, may well be Minnie's father, unwittingly incestuous in his desire for her. During this exchange, Johnny's language is in the "Indian manner," highlighting the difference between himself and the white man he addresses:

"That girl you spoke to is Indian girl – straight Indian. Her mother was daughter of a chief; her father don't matter – he was nothing."

"What about her father?" the white man asked, insolently.

"Her father don't count," said Johnny, slowly, "he was just yellow dog of white man, the kind we see some time at the hotel – fresh guy that talks too much." (144)

This exchange and the information it conveys about Minnie's parentage has the effect of silencing the "portly gentleman," but it also sets in motion his desire for revenge. When, however, the "stranger" apologizes, linguistic "whiteness" returns to Johnny, who answers the white man's nervous – and, we are to see by the twitching of his "flabby hands" (155), guilty – questions about Minnie in an articulate manner. "Her mother was one of the chief's daughters," says Johnny, "and she was born here nineteen years ago, I think" (155). "No one," he goes on, "knows much about [her father]" (155). Johnny's language here is in marked contrast to his excited and "broken" outburst in the dining room: here the "training and education" are in the ascendant, and the "savagery" contained. It is, however, "released" through the application of liquor by the white man.

As in "Babette," white men who do not behave "like white folks" are configured as the basis for social problems. They remind us that empires fall, as McClung put it in *In Times Like These*, because of too much "masculinity" (147). The white man who wants to seduce Minnie epitomizes white vice of the kind McClung always foregrounds as the greatest inhibitor of the Anglo-Saxon civilizing mission. This man represents the kind of ruiner of innocent girls McClung treats to such invective in *Painted Fires*, in which the girls at the Friendly Home are shown to have ended up there largely through their exploitation and abandonment by men. This representation reflects a purity argument in circulation at least from the 1880s when the existence of a white slave trade to satisfy male lust was scandalously publicized and adopted into the popular rhetoric of the causes and effects of Anglo-Saxon racial degeneration. In "Red and White," Minnie hates the white man not only because he is obviously trying to seduce her but because he is – or at least reminds her of – the father for whom she has already indicated her lack of affection. "There was something in the tone of the stranger's voice," we learn, "a sort of vaseline softness, that stirred bitter memories" (141). The man has already been set up as potentially the father of nineteen-year-old Minnie (165) when he tells his companion that he had been at this same spot ("virgin wilderness the last time [he] saw it") "out hunting for a week" nineteen years earlier. "That was the time," he reminisces, "a fellow could have a good time; there were no laws, no ten commandments, and no consequences ... The Indians were in great form. They took us up the lake in canoes, and showed us how to tan hides and make moccasins. There were some pretty girls among them, with shy brown eyes and red cheeks" (140). "That girl," he continues, pointing at Minnie serving the next table "reminds me of one of them – same carriage and same dignified manner. By Jove! she *is* a pretty girl" (140–1).

Although the man is represented as being a racist, the narrative suggests that his racism is rooted in sexism. He resents the Christianizing and Canadianizing work that is performed at the mission schools through the intervention of white women like the teacher Miss Bowden. When Minnie rejects his advances, he directs his animosity obliquely towards the white women and "home missions" workers whom he sees at work in the West to the detriment of the fulfilment of his own desires. "It's all a part of this damned uplift business!" he snarls (143), referring both to the "uplift" of indigenous Canadians and, less obviously, to the "uplift" of women, both through feminist activism: "There is no place where a man has any liberty any more. Here, even here in this neck of the woods, the half-breed girls after a year or two in these infernal industrial schools get the airs of a duchess, and imbibe notions entirely beyond their place ... I'll bet that black-eyed jade wants to vote, and all the rest of it. A real man might as well be dead as live in this world when the bars go and every last woman is of this independent kind" (143). McClung's politics here anticipate second-wave ideas of global sisterhood, while remaining entrenched in first-wave ideologies of "race." Her sense is that the "black-eyed jade" *should* vote, because she would "naturally" work against the continued destructive "liberty" of men such as this one.

It is difficult to say how McClung, who died in 1951, would have responded to the exclusion of First Nations peoples from the federal franchise in Canada until 1960. It is also difficult to imagine how she would have reacted to the reports of the abuses in residential schools and of the schools' function as arguably genocidal.[11] In one sense she was an obvious part of the problem, in that she supported the schools and fostered, with stories like "Red and White" and "Babette" and with eugenical ideas of race and nation, the cultural climate that maintained native disenfranchisement. In another sense, however, it is not entirely fair to disregard McClung's own ideologically constrained struggles with questions of race and rights. She spoke out on more than one occasion after World War I against restricting the numbers of immigrants permitted into Canada, and against the xenophobic attitudes underpinning the push for such restriction (Davis and Hallett, 1994, 274). At that time she also made clear her position that the right to vote should not be racially determined.[12] While she did not take up aboriginal enfranchisement as a public cause, she does indicate in "Red and White" and in "Babette" that her notion of suffrage had come to include all women. She would make this point in her public writing, however, with reference not to aboriginal women but to immigrant women. Although she is famously noted as having written to Prime Minister Borden before the extending of the franchise to women that it was needed to "right the balance" (Savage 1985, 134), she wrote in *In Times Like These* against the "fear that the granting of woman suffrage would greatly increase the unintelligent vote, because the foreign women would then have the franchise, and in our blind egotism we class our foreign people as ignorant people, if they do not know our ways and our language. They may know many other languages, but if they have not yet mastered ours they are poor, ignorant foreigners" (76–7). She would maintain this position. Davis and Hallett describe a speech made some twenty years later, in 1936, on behalf of British Columbia cabinet minister Ian Mackenzie, when McClung "stated her belief that Japanese Canadians had the right to vote: 'I believe that every human has a right to vote. I could not take the responsibility of claiming for myself a privilege I wouldn't give to anybody else'" (1994, 274).

It is, "Red and White" suggests, albeit with considerable ambivalence, a right McClung would have liked to have seen extended to indigenous women – although, it is clear, along the racial axis that determined her vision for the nation of Canada within the empire of Great Britain. That is, this story, along with "Babette," also suggests that the construction of all women as citizens was a matter of inculcation into a white, middle-class model of maternalist womanhood, determined and implemented by white, middle-class, maternalist women, those who had been called by the imperatives of eugenics as the last best measure for the preservation of "the race."

Epilogue

We Anglo-Saxon people have a decided sense of our own superiority,
and we feel sure that our skin is exactly the right color, and we people
from Huron and Bruce feel sure that we were born in the right place,
too. So we naturally look down upon those who happen to be of a
different race and tongue than our own.

McClung, 1915

At the 1999 unveiling of the Famous Five statues in Calgary, Adrienne
Clarkson suggested that Emily Murphy "would have been thrilled
today to see that there was not only a woman senator, and a number
of them, dozens of them, but a Chinese woman senator and a Chinese Governor General" (*Edmonton Journal*, 19 October, 1999).
Columnists such as Naomi Lakritz objected to Clarkson's specula-
tion, but there is a good deal of evidence to suggest that both
Murphy and McClung were well aware of what they saw as their
period's racism and were troubled by it. Murphy is always quoted
on the "fertile yellow races" and of having called Chinese men
"traitors and 'men of fishy blood who might easily be guilty of any
enormity no matter how villainous'" (ibid.); she is less frequently
noted for having taken a position *against* contemporary popular
ideas in English Canada. She wrote in 1932, "Speaking of colors
recalls to mind how social alarmists are won't [sic] to affright us
with what they are pleased to call 'the yellow peril,' just as if a
deeper pigment of the skin precluded the Chinese, Hindus and
Japanese from the benefits of civic rights and the Christian religion"
(*Vancouver Sun*, 1 October 1932).

Murphy's argument here is obviously, like McClung's for the vote
for "foreign women," still limited in its perception of "civic rights."
This passage, after all, occurs in her most extensive public case for
eugenical sterilization. It does, however, suggest that the selective

quoting from Murphy's work that characterizes her and McClung's recent treatment by the Canadian media could be balanced to show both women confronting and countering at least some of their own contemporary ideologies of race and nation.

The contradictions that critics and historians have seen in first-wave "maternal" feminism are certainly in evidence in McClung's own politics. "Red and White" and "Babette" are perceptible as racist narratives, working to implement assimilationist ideas, based on stereotypical notions of indigeneity, and represented as an effect of the eugenic work of the imperial mother who is delineated in so much of McClung's fiction. They are also – particularly "Babette" – arguably struggling to see outside of their contemporary ideological frame, even as they demonstrate their concern with facilitating Anglo-Saxon settlement and imperial regeneration in the West through the work of women. McClung shows signs of similar struggles in much of her writing. She supported open-door policies of immigration at a time when many Canadians saw "foreigners" flooding the labour pool ("We Must Share"). She indicated on other occasions that conflict between the white settler culture and non-Anglo-Saxon immigrants was the result of white prejudice: "If the foreigners of Canada are to be taught to be loyal they must have something to be loyal to, and the best thing to be loyal to is a friend. We want to teach them to love our flag, but the only way to make them love the flag, is to make them love us. Legislation won't take the place of neighborliness; we need a new spirit in our people" (*Maclean's*, July 1919, 93).[1] This sentiment is of course still based on the binarized sense of Canadian "us" and foreign "them" that characterizes early twentieth-century notions of "birthright" and what one commentator called "the Canadian Canadian" (Hawkes, 1919). But it is also arguably indicative of a kind of thinking *against* the period's racism.

Nellie L. McClung was a supporter of eugenics, and eugenical thinking informs every aspect of her feminism and social reform, her fiction, and her vision "of a better world." This study has been concerned precisely with the eugenical nature of her work and how she undertook to disseminate and implement eugenic ideas and policies of gender, race, nation, and empire through her fiction as the primary tool of her reform. This has been undertaken not for purposes of national memorialization nor continued feminist recuperation but to consider what it means to read McClung's work through the eugenical ideas with which she is now associated first; to understand how and why she continues to hold such a prominent and conflicted position in the discourses of nationalism and the narratives of national history; and to begin to trace not the differences but some of the points of a continuum between "first-wave" and contemporary "third-wave" feminism in English Canada.

As McClung's work and writings so clearly demonstrate, western feminism is embedded in the history and the politics of imperialism. Moreover, a century later it is still configured in terms of the ideas of social evolution that were the primary rationale across discursive fields for empire: empire was the inevitable result of the forward movement of "civilization." Feminists in the early twenty-first century are understood to be perceptually more "advanced" than the suffrage feminists ("we" see "their" shortcomings), and that is why is it often seen to be important to distance contemporary feminism from its history. Indeed, much contemporary feminism – or feminist analysis, at any rate – is primarily concerned with the critique of its own history, and with the marking of distance from at least the white and Anglo-Saxon predecessors ("foremothers" for the second wave, but not for the third). For the third wave, this history is a preoccupation that often obviates contemporary gender inequities and thus works to convey a sense that many of the inequities of "the past" have been resolved. There is a sense that feminism has other issues to address than those that were the focus of activism and reform from the 1960s to the 1980s. It is harder now to find ways to talk about the problems, for instance, of patriarchy, the oppression of women in a range of national and cultural and social locations, gender-based sexual violence, the poverty of single mothers, equal pay for work of equal value, the tenuous hold of women in North America on freedom of choice with regard to birth control, access to abortion, access to daycare, maternity leave, support for teenage mothers after their children are born, ideologies and politics of maternity, work and child raising, legal rights, and gender-based repression in some régimes. Third-wave self-reflexivity is underpinned not only by a desire to disavow the racialized politics of early twentieth-century feminism but by a notion that many of the "old" issues of feminism no longer need to be considered – that second-wave activist feminism (like the Cold War that to some extent is its cultural context) is obsolete because those goals have been achieved.

But this notion – of progress – is itself an indication of the extent to which western feminism is still invested in a theory of upward social movement, marked by women and women's position in society, precisely the same theory articulated by McClung in *In Times Like These* and by other late nineteenth and early twentieth-century feminists. The question is not "How far have we come?" as in the second wave, but "How has feminist ideology changed?"

The notion that the third wave has gone beyond the "racism" of earlier feminism needs to be reconsidered, in part by understanding it in the work of writers such as McClung, from whom third-wave commentators have sought to distance themselves at the same moment that national rhetoric has valorized her as a hero. The tension between the two positions is obvious. Also importantly, the notion that western feminism always *only* participates in a patriarchal and imperial construction of subjectivity or agency through the disempowerment of racialized others needs to be addressed. Feminism – even feminism like McClung's, which is so clearly a discourse of imperialism and a technology of empire – is not monolithic. To attend to its complexities is not to deny a history and a continuum of just such disempowerment – in which McClung is certainly complicit – and not to move a western constituency of women "forward," but to continue to clarify the historical shifts in gender and power that feminism has produced, the variants between kinds of feminist agency, and the pressures that affect gender politics in different contexts and at different times.

Notes

INTRODUCTION

1 Candace Savage notes: "Late in 1916, when the prime minister,
  Sir Robert Borden, was visiting the West, [McClung had] taken the
  opportunity to buttonhole him" and urge him to "advance the federal franchise to British and Canadian women" with enlisted relatives (134; see also Davis and Hallett, 1994, 151). As Davis and
  Hallett point out, "This proposal was not well received by most suffrage workers," who objected to the exclusion of non-British and
  Anglo-Canadian women from this limited franchise. McClung with-
  drew her proposal for an act that would thus racially limit the
  female vote (as it would also ultimately limit the male vote) in
  Canada. She wrote a letter to the *Grain Growers' Guide* withdraw-
  ing "the suggestion of a partial franchise" (151). On the Wartime
  Elections Act of 1917, see Cleverdon, especially 124, 129–30.
2 The "Famous Five" were McClung, Henrietta Muir Edwards, Louise
  McKinney, Emily Murphy, and Irene Parlby.
3 McClung writes at the end of the introduction to *The Stream Runs
  Fast* (in part, cited as epigraph here), "still, I cannot look back without regret. I can see too many places where I could have been more
  obedient to the heavenly vision, for a vision I surely had for the creation of a better world. But I hope I am leaving at least some small
  legacy of truth" (1945, xiii).

4 The Scrapbook *Hansard* for the Alberta Legislature records on 25 February 1922 that McClung and Irene Parlby responded angrily to "the question of allowing married women whose husbansd [sic] were earning a good living wage, to take positions under the [Minimum Wage] act, except in times like the war when other labor was scarce" (*Hansard*, 2 February 1922–12 April 1924, 27).

5 Fiamengo, "A Legacy of Ambivalence: Responses to Nellie McClung": 70–87.

6 The CRB Foundation was established in 1986 by Andrea and Charles Bronfman in Montreal, to "foster the unity of the Jewish people whose soul is in Jerusalem, and enhance Canadianism" ("Funders Online: The CRB Foundation," European Foundation Centre, December 1998; February 2005.)

7 See, for instance, "100 Most Important Canadians in History," *Maclean's*, 1 July 1998, and Dominion Institute/Council for Canadian Unity, "Celebrating and Understanding Our Heroes: Canada's Top 20 Heroes As Chosen by Canadians," 1999. The latter list was drawn from a web-based survey of 28,000 people.

8 English-Canadian historians have noted for many years that first-wave feminists and women's groups in Alberta fought for the 1928 bill, but the reports of the Muir trial brought this information to the foreground and significantly altered popular perceptions of Murphy and McClung.

9 For instance, a *Canadian Press Newswire* of 27 June 1995 noted Gerald Robertson's expert testimony that "Alberta's women's advocates Emily Murphy and Nellie McClung also supported the creation of a sterilization law." Another *CP Newswire* on 23 June had similarly drawn attention to the fact that early Canadian champions of eugenics "also included Emily Murphy, Louise McKinney and Nellie McClung, whose portraits hang on a wall ... just down the hallway from where Muir's case is being tried in the Law Courts building."

10 Compare this to another *Western Report* comment that, "Among the greatest eugenics supporters were the Women's [sic] Christian Temperance Union and suffragettes like Nellie McClung" (9, no. 22 [1993]: 38).

11 See also McLaren 1990, chapter 1.

12 These statistics are prefigured in comments such as Murphy's in a 1932 article entitled "Sterilization of the Insane": "The only portion of the British Empire which has officially adopted permissive

eugenical sterilization of the insane and feeble-minded is the Province of Alberta ... You are quite right: Alberta prefers to lead the followers rather than to follow the leaders. To forestall any would-be wits, permit me to say that 70% of Alberta's insane are not natives of this, the newest province in Confederation, but come from countries outside of Canada" (*Vancouver Sun*, 3 September 1932, 3).

13 See for instance *Alberta Report* 25, no. 22 (1999): 38: "But She Was a Feminist Racist: A Columnist Has Some Startling Words about the Famous Five."

14 See also *Calgary Herald*, 19 October 1999, A1, "Statues Salute Trail-Blazing Women," and *Edmonton Journal*, 19 October 1999, A7, "Clarkson Salutes Famous Five."

15 Murphy may have taken this reference to Saleeby from *Maclean's*. In January 1920, *Maclean's* reported Saleeby's "alarming fact" that "for the first time on record the deaths (in the last quarter of 1918 and first of 1919) have actually exceeded the births!" It also noted: "There are more Germans in Germany to-day than there are Britons in the whole extent of our world-wide Empire" (46).

16 This case rehearsed the concerns that had been expressed nearly a decade earlier with regard to the naming of a government building in Toronto after Clara Brett Martin, the first woman called to the bar in Canada. In that case opponents drew attention to Martin's anti-Semitism, arguing that it would be inappropriate and offensive to publicly commemorate her. The building, like SAGE House, was renamed. See Ghosh, *Catholic New Times* 23, no. 15 (1999): 10–11.

17 The investment of first-wave feminism in the construction of a white, Anglo-Saxon, and Protestant Canada where a new and better "race" would flourish has been well documented in accounts of the woman suffrage movement in English Canada. Studies such as Carol Lee Bacchi's 1983 monograph, *Liberation Deferred? The Ideas of the English-Canadian Suffragists, 1877–1918*, and Mariana Valverde's important article in 1992, "'When the Mother of the Race Is Free': Race, Reproduction, and Sexuality in First-Wave Feminism," have drawn attention to what Bacchi configures as the "unifying theme" in the suffrage movement: the tendentious strand of all first-wave politics, she suggests, was "a concern for the future of the Anglo-Saxon race" (1983, 104). British and American studies have similarly problematized first-wave feminism, and, in particular, suffragism in those contexts as a politics of women's "advancement"

that is embedded in ideas of racial "progress." Other writers have
shown how British feminism is fundamentally and inextricably
linked with the ideologies of late nineteenth and early twentieth
century imperialism as, in Charles Dilke's words, a "conception" of
"the grandeur of our race" and a concomitant conception of evolutionary shortcomings in non-Anglo Saxons: Vron Ware in *Beyond
the Pale: White Women, Racism and History* (1992); Nupur
Chaudhuri and Margaret Strobel in *Western Women and Imperialism: Complicity and Resistance* (1993); Antoinette Burton in
*Burdens of History: British Feminists, Indian Women, and Impe-
rial Culture, 1865–1915* (1994); Kumari Jayawardena in *The
White Woman's Other Burden: Western Women and South Asia
during British Colonial Rule* (1995); and Anne McClintock in *Imperial Leather: Race, Gender, and Sexuality in the Colonial Contest*
(1995). Lucy Bland's *Banishing the Beast: Sexuality and the Early
Feminists* (1995) has been particularly influential in foregrounding
the ways in which British feminism must be understood in the context of imperial ideas of race and reproduction. Numerous studies
continue to follow these works. In 1998 the Manchester University
Press Studies in Imperialism series produced a collection of essays on
Gender and Imperialism, edited by Clare Midgley; in 1999, Indiana
University Press published a collection edited by Ruth Roach Pierson
and Nupur Chaudhuri, *Nation, Empire, Colony: Historicizing
Gender and Race*. Both books present a range of historical essays on
questions of feminism in national and imperial contexts that collectively problematize the notion of national and imperial feminism as
a liberatory politics and an unassailable position of moral rectitude.
These studies demonstrate that first-wave feminism is not something
that occurred in *reaction* to imperialism but *within* it; white women
cannot occupy the position of "the colonized" because their own
work – suffrage, missionary, social purity activist – was crucial to
imperial colonization. White women, these studies have shown,
achieved "advancement" through the construction of categories of
subordinate and needy alterity, exactly as empire itself made its
"progress" across the globe. As Burton has argued, "In historical
terms, middle-class liberal feminism was one of the manifestations of
British cultural hegemony as well as one of the technologies of
British imperial power" (19). Feminism in imperial Canada must
also be seen to be one of these "technologies."

18 McLaren notes that "in Alberta, between 1928 and 1972, 4,725 cases were proposed for sterilization and 2,822 approved" (1990, 159).

19 Ted Byfield makes the point in the *Alberta Report* that eugenical work in Alberta "was advanced by social activists and reformers, the forebears of modern liberaldom, and vigorously resisted by religious conservatives – Catholics, evangelical Protestants, Orthodox and some Anglicans" (26, no. 25 [1999]: 44).

20 See, for instance, Georgina Murray, "Agonize, Don't Organize: A Critique of Postfeminism" (1997). Murray maintains that "Postfeminist theory has disconnected women from activism in the name of difference; their idea of difference admirably recognizes that women have different needs but then deprives them of a common commitment to end female oppression. Postfeminist difference means that as women we have no voice because we speak for no one" (37).

21 University of Toronto Press reissued the 1921 suffrage novel *Purple Springs* in 1992, with a new introduction by Randi R. Warne. Marilyn I. Davis produced a selection of short fiction under the title *Stories Subversive: Through the Fields with Gloves Off*, published by University of Ottawa Press in 1998. In 2003, Broadview Press Canada published McClung's autobiography.

22 See Bacchi, Cleverdon, Strong-Boag, and Valverde.

PART ONE

1 Although McClung did not speak in England for the suffrage cause, she had, as Marilyn I. Davis and Mary Hallett have noted, met Emmeline Pankhurst in Winnipeg in 1911 (118–19) and maintained contact with her, later seeing her in Edmonton. *In Times Like These* was published by Appleton in New York in 1915 and by McLeod and Allen in Toronto in the same year. It was reissued by McLeod and Allen in 1919.

2 See especially Lucy Bland 1995, 70; see also Carol Bacchi, Catherine Cleverdon, Wayne Roberts, and Mariana Valverde.

3 Compare to Charlotte Perkins Gilman, *The Man-Made World* (1911): "The basic feminine impulse is to gather, to put together, to construct; the basic masculine impulse to scatter, to disseminate, to destroy" (1911 [1971], 114).

4 The "first wave" in English Canada cannot be assigned rigid boundaries. As an organized movement, working for suffrage and

equal rights for women, it emerges in the 1880s and ends, more or less, with the Second World War.

5 See, for instance, Valverde: "Women without children, as well as those in traditional family situations, justified their claims to political and social rights by reference to their quasi-maternal public and private roles" (1992, 3).

6 Ardis's *New Woman, New Novel* has been one of the most influential of these studies. Misao Dean's account of the New Woman in Canada in *Practising Femininity* is one part of her important study of English-Canadian women's writing.

7 Bland notes that the term "feminist" does not circulate until 1895 (1987, 142).

8 On the New Woman's positioning as a catalyst of imperial decline, see C. Devereux, 1999: 175–84.

9 See Davin 1978, 15–16.

10 These dangers to reproduction are usually the domain of middle-class women, for whom education was possible and work outside the home was unusual. Working-class and poor women were, conversely, constructed as objects of middle-class female attention.

11 "The race," as Lawson, for instance, argued, "has not yet reached its acme of development, its highest state of unfoldment. It is surely climbing upward, but it has now reached a point whence it can climb no higher until it makes more moral progress; until it throws off its burden of oppression of man against man, and man against woman. There can be no further advancement until … woman take[s] her rightful place in the world as man's recognised equal" (1990, 118–19).

12 Strachey cites J.A. Hobson's figures from his 1902 book, *Imperialism*, demonstrating that Britain acquired "a territory of 4,754,000 square miles" between 1870 and 1900 (79).

13 See Devereux, 2000: 1–23.

14 Carolyn Burdett has similarly observed, "When women were addressed, by eugenic discourse, as maternal, they were at the same time interpellated as mothers *for* the nation. When women defined themselves as social and ethical agents, they simultaneously positioned themselves within a national context" (48).

15 Lucy Bland similarly suggests that feminists "appropriated" the maternal ideas of eugenics (1995, 222–49).

16 In a speech delivered after the Second World War on the radio (it is entitled in its typescript version in the Provincial Archives of British

Columbia simply "Radio"), McClung said, "We used to hear about the New Woman. I seem to remember a phrase which attended her – Women's Rights. Today the new woman is out of fashion and we need a Woman, who is really new because radically remade from within. *This* new woman will not think of rights but of responsibilities. She will be distinguished by the depth and power of her feeling: her emotions, instead of being repressed, will be freed and directed" (PABC MS-0100, box 25, file 8: 6)

At this point, it is difficult to tell if McClung is referring to the 1890s New Woman or to what she had designated, in Pearlie Watson, in the first three decades of the century as the New Woman who fought for "Women's Rights." What is clear, however, is McClung's sense that the New Woman, to be feminist, and to effect social change, needed to be less individualist.

17 The imputing of agency to first-wave feminists is the crux of the difference between second- and third-wave perceptions, particularly of the extent to which the first wave invested in the ideas of race preservation and eugenics. The view of the first wave from the 1960s to the 1980s, more or less, was that women *had* to capitulate to prevailing ideas, even if they did not want to, in order to advance their cause. The more recent perception is that they were complicit in the work of ethnic nationalism and imperialism and "leaders" of legislation such as Alberta's Sexual Sterilization Bill.

18 When Havelock Ellis took up the question of the transmission of "ability" in his 1904 *Study of British Genius*, he would not diverge significantly from Galton in situating "genius" in men. "A slightly lower standard of ability, it would appear," he wrote in the introduction to a later edition, "prevails among the women than among the men" (1904, 9).

19 See Burdett, 47–53. For an extensive discussion of Pearson and the Men and Women's Club, see Bland's *Banishing the Beast* (1995), 3–47.

20 British doctor Mary Scharlieb was the first woman to graduate M.D. from London University (in 1888) and the "first woman to hold a staff appointment in a London general hospital" (DNB 1937, 750). In 1912 she published a short analysis, *Womanhood and Race-Regeneration*, in a eugenical series "promoted," we are told on the flyleaf, "by the National Council of Public Morals, Holborn Hall, W.C." This series, which appeared under the general heading "New Tracts for the Times," included works by Havelock Ellis (*The*

Problem of Race-Regeneration) and Saleeby (*The Methods of Race Regeneration*), as well as by another widely read eugenist, Arthur Newsholme (*The Declining Birth-Rate – Its National and International Significance*).

Although Scharlieb was a well-known suffragist (Bland 1995, 232), her discussion was not directly engaged with feminist issues but with eugenical ones. Her contribution to the series sought to define women's work within the eugenical project, and began with what was by 1912 a fairly conventional eugenist argument: "It is no exaggeration to say that on woman depends the welfare of the race, for not only is she the parent most intimately in contact with the growing child, but her influence is generally paramount both with her husband and with her grown-up family. It is merely a truism that the race will be whatever the women of the race make it" (5).

Scharlieb then presented a case for the training of women *as* mothers, through both the educational apparatus that had come by 1907 to be known as "mothercraft" and more general education. Women's "brains are as good and clear" as men's, she argued, but their duty to the race was different; higher education "and degrees" for women should be "prized not as ends in themselves, but as the means whereby untold benefit is to be conferred on the race ... This intellectual power is held in trust to pass on the great gift to the next generation, to her own children should she be so fortunate as to be a mother, to the children of others should that crown of womanhood pass her by" (11).

Not quite feminist, Scharlieb's argument is also not quite *not* feminist: its opening dictum aligns it with the stance taken by suffrage feminists like McClung and Gilman, that "the race will be whatever the women of the race make it," and with Schreiner that "all women ought to be trained ... that they should cease to be parasites" (Scharlieb 1912, 37). Her sense of women's "intellectual power" counters the Galtonian conception of uniquely male "ability" and the position that women should not be educated, and establishes a basis – indeed, a necessity – for comprehending intellectual and social equality *within* a framework of sexual difference and different duties. She concluded, "It is only as the woman realises her equality with man that she can become her best self and develop to the utmost her powers of regenerating and raising the race" (52).

La Reine Helen Baker took a comparable position in her 1912 volume, *Race Improvement and Eugenics: A Little Book on a Great Subject*. In a chapter on "Eugenics and the Modern Feminist

Movement," she maintained that the "woman movement aims at removing the obstacles" to eugenical marriage between equals, and arises, as McClung would also suggest, as a natural, *moral* response to the increasing degeneration caused by "male statecraft": "The tragedy of the woman's life is when either her own or her husband's unfitness to bear anything but a tainted stock is disregarded by law, custom and the brutality of lustful bestiality. She who might be, *as she desires to be*, the guardian of the nation's truest interest, is overpowered and compelled to be the medium of national pollution. This knowledge strengthens the women's agitation; the determination to end such a shameful degradation makes the woman's movement irresistible" (99–100, emphasis added).

Moreover, she argued, as Gilman had, by implication, in "The Yellow Wall Paper," that "apart from the maternal side of woman's life there is her individual life to consider, and while this is of enormous importance to herself its chief interest to Eugenists (as such) is that only out of healthy and happy conditions of womanhood can a noble motherhood be expected to grow" (96).

21 Janice Fiamengo notes that "McClung's signature is conspicuously absent from letters sent in support of the Sterilization Act [and] she is not on record as speaking in favour of the act in the Legislature" (85n11). McClung, indeed, hardly spoke of eugenics directly, her comments on the popular misapprehensions of the movement in the 1919 *Everywoman's World* article "Listen – Ladies" being a relatively rare taking up of the term itself. Indeed, she makes few explicit references to the term. One notable reference occurs in relation to the mating habits of beavers, who, she notes, "separate at the end of the first year, by some inexorable eugenic law, all the males going upstream and the females downstream" (*Leaves from Lantern Lane*, 5). The support of eugenics, however, is evident in her feminist and nationalist vocabulary of race preservation and regeneration, as well as in policies she proposes.

22 The Scrapbook *Hansard* for the Alberta Legislature does not indicate that McClung was one of the speakers who addressed the bill. It is also worth noting that McClung did not include the bill in an account of what she later felt she had been part of accomplishing in the 1920s in Alberta.

23 The *Hansard* record of debate of the legislative assembly in Alberta for the duration of McClung's tenure as a member and through the discussions of the Sexual Sterilization Bill is in scrapbook form.

24 Bland is citing Mary Haweis.

PART TWO

1 See James Hammerton 1979 and 1977; see also Barbara Roberts. Susan Jackel's *A Flannel Shirt and Liberty: British Emigrant Gentlewomen in the Canadian West, 1880–1914* collects a range of contemporary documents: Jessie M. Saxby's 1890 "Women Wanted" (66–74) is noteworthy. Jackel also reproduces the 1886 CPR pamphlet, *What Women Say of the Canadian North-West* (31–65).

2 See Amirah Inglis's *The White Woman's Protection Ordinance: Sexual Anxiety and Politics in Papua* (1975) and, with reference to the Canadian context, Sarah Carter's *Capturing Women*, and Constance Backhouse's discussion of the White Woman's Labour Law in *Colour-Coded: A Legal History of Racism in Canada* (1999).

3 See Inglis, *The White Woman's Protection Ordinance* (1975). On "The White Woman's Labour Law," see Backhouse 1999, 132–72, and Carter 1997, 198.

4 See Burton's *Burdens of History* (1994), especially 1–32, and her earlier essay "The White Woman's Burden: British Feminists and 'The Indian Woman,' 1865–1915" in Chaudhuri and Strobel 1992 (137–57).

5 Janice Fiamengo has suggested that this notion of maternalism shows McClung configuring gender across racial divides: "By mobilizing the ethical power of motherhood, McClung could extend, even to many non-Anglo-Saxon women, the right to full participation in public affairs" (76).

6 McClung's comments on the exclusion of the "pioneer woman" from history are an important reminder of the processes of gender construction within ideological state apparatuses.

7 The notion of the West as the "Land of the Second Chance," the "Land of Beginning Again," is most powerfully in evidence in the second novel of the Watson trilogy, *The Second Chance* (1910), but it is also fundamental to McClung's representation of Canada as "The Land of the Fair Deal" in *In Times Like These*. (See especially pages 157–61.) The poem with which the book ends configures the West as "the sunset sky" that "show[s] us that a day may die/ With greater glory than it's born" (218). In *The Black Creek Stopping-House*, McClung suggests that the perception of the West as a pure and purifying site is a "delusion" (25).

    The marriage of the Brydons is also suggestively allegorical. Like the marriage in Sara Jeannette Duncan's *Cousin Cinderella* (1908), what is brought together, here in the context of the West, the "Land of Beginning Again," is the best of British manhood and of the progeny of self-made Canadian manhood, identified as imperial in the name of the lumber company with which Mr Robert Grant makes his fortune.

8 See Devereux 2001: 6–22 and 2004, Introduction, *Anne of Green Gables* (Broadview).

9 McClung's publisher commented in 1908 that they could not keep up with demand. The editors of the story anthology *New Women* have suggested that initially *Sowing Seeds in Danny* outsold *Anne of Green Gables* in Canada.

10 The other four works cited by Logan and French are L.M. Montgomery's *Anne of Green Gables*, Marian Keith's *Duncan Polite* (actually published in 1905), *Little Stories of Quebec* by James Le Rossingnol, and Marjorie Pickthall's short story "La Tristesse," in the *Atlantic Monthly* (299).

11 See Devereux 2001.

12 See *New Women: Short Stories by Canadian Women.*

13 See, for instance, Marjorie MacMurchy, *The Woman, Bless Her: Not As Amiable a Book As It Sounds.*

14 This story is included in the 1974 collection, *The Road to Yesterday* (131–74).

15 I have not located a book with this author and title. McClung is probably alluding to the enormous number of "manuals" instructing women about motherhood.

16 The novel was published in Britain under the title *Danny and the Pink Lady* (1908, Hodder and Stoughton).

17 Marilla Cuthbert, in Montgomery's *Anne of Green Gables*, undergoes a similarly maternal "awakening." See Devereux 2001.

18 I am indebted to Kate Flint for drawing Mangum's work to my attention.

19 McClung was not the only English-Canadian woman writer of the early twentieth century who would undertake the work of construct-ing the mother of the race through narratives of exemplary conver-sion and eugenical marriage. L.M. Montgomery's "Anne" books arguably took up the same ideological project in the narrativizing of Anne Shirley's growth as a mother; even Sara Jeannette Duncan, in the first decade or so of the century, would engage with the idea of the woman as mother and the implications for "the race" of women's failure to mobilize the "maternal instinct." Duncan's 1904

story "A Mother in India" shows her problematizing the question of reproductive duty and the biological "instinct," and her 1905 novel *Cousin Cinderella* shows her to have invested to some extent in the ideas of imperial renewal through eugenical unions allegorized as romantic marriage. McClung produces such an allegory in *The Second Chance*, in the story of the union of Martha Perkins, whom we are to see as embodying the country (1910, 369), with Arthur Wemyss, the good Englishman who has come to Canada to learn farming. The son of a bishop, Arthur is shown to come of "good stock," which, however, like the stock from which Lord Peter comes in Duncan's *Cousin Cinderella*, needs a regenerative boost. Such a boost in this case can only be provided by the solid, hard-working, maternal, and Canadian Martha. The eponymous second chance is thus not only the Watsons' or Sandy Braden's or even lovelorn Martha's, but the empire's, since the progeny of this union promises to be the "best" of new and old. The imperial allegory is config- ured in more explicitly national terms in the conclusion of the Watson trilogy as a whole, when mother-of-the-race Pearl finally unites with the young salt-of-the earth doctor Horace Clay. The "real empire-builders," as McClung describes the Watsons, are to be found, as Duncan also suggests, amongst the Anglo-Saxon "stock" on the frontiers.

PART THREE

1 See, for example, a monograph published in Nova Scotia in 1911 by the Tri-County Anti Tuberculosis League (11), or C.W. Saleeby's 1921 outline of what he called *The Eugenic Prospect*; part 3 (151–80) is entitled "The White Plague." One work to deploy this term as something with overtly racial overtones is the 1952 study by René and Jean Dubos, *The White Plague: Tuberculosis, Man and Society*.

2 Douglas Fetherling has used this term to refer to the kind of popular writing that appeared in English-Canadian periodicals in the early twentieth century. See the *Toronto Star*, 10 February 1996, H1–2.

3 Carol Bacchi also makes the point that a "social élite" in Britain saw Canada as "a regenerative force within the Empire" (1983, 105).

4 The natural curative potential of the western part of the continent was a matter for some debate. Huber, for instance, in a chapter on

"The 'Lunger' in the West," argues that the many sanataria that sprang up in the West to meet popular demand were simply exploiting the ill without curing them in any special way. "The climate of the West," he concludes, "is not essential to recovery from consumption, and ... sufferers are quite as likely to get well near their own homes in the East" (128).

5 Sheila M. Rothman has noted the emergence of a similar rhetoric with regard to the "purity" of the American West in the second half of the nineteenth century (131–47).

6 Saleeby claims that Newsholme wrote *The Prevention of Tuberculosis* at his request (1921, 153).

7 *Sowing Seeds in Danny* remained in print until the 1970s. *Purple Springs* was issued as a reprint with an introduction by Randi R. Warne by University of Toronto Press in 1992.

8 Valverde notes that Christabel Pankhurst published a pamphlet on syphilis in 1913 in Britain called *The Great Scourge and How to End It* (Valverde 1991, 24). The *Oxford English Dictionary* indicates that tuberculosis is also characterized as the "white scourge."

9 See, for instance, Deborah Gorham (1976).

10 Valverde (1991, 24n28) is citing Pankhurst's anti-venereal disease pamphlet, *The Great Scourge and How to End It*.

11 George Moore's *Esther Waters*, for instance, makes this link implicit in its tuberculosis narrative.

12 The tubercle bacillus was discovered in 1881 by Robert Koch, who published his findings in 1882 in *The Etiology of Tuberculosis*.

13 It is worth noting that in the late twentieth and early twenty-first centuries in North America, the social reform focus on alcohol and children has shifted to women, who are reminded in government-sponsored advertisements of the dangers alcohol represents to a foetus.

14 The same logic pertained to varying degrees throughout Canada. See Katherine McCuaig (1999), who has commented that "it was eminently logical for reformers, such as Emily Murphy, a pioneer in the anti-TB movement, to work simultaneously for prohibition, women's suffrage, and a myriad of other reform causes" (12).

15 See Newsholme 1908, 121–45; Huber 1906, 63–5; Saleeby 1921, 152–3.

16 McClung writes of the Watson family in *Purple Springs*: "They had been and were, the real Empire-builders who subdued the soil and

made it serve human needs, enduring hardships and hunger and cold and bitter discouragements, always with heroism and patience" (1992, 72).

17 In warmer climates, tents were often dispensed with altogether. Sara Jeannette Duncan, for instance, who had tuberculosis, describes a summer passed outside in a Simla garden in her 1901 autobiographical book, *On the Other Side of the Latch*.

18 See Katherine McCuaig (1999), who points out that by 1942, "37.2 percent of the patients in Canadian sanatoria had some form of collapse therapy" (197).

19 See, for example, Inge, cited in the Tri-County manual: "A certificate of sound health should be one of the things insisted upon before marriage" (121). Huber begins his chapter on "Marriage and the Offspring" with this grim epigraph: "Many a young man has sacrificed his chances of recovery on the altar of Hymen" (171).

20 See Warne's introduction to *Purple Springs* (1992) for a discussion of the Women's Parliament represented in the novel.

21 Palmer points out that "Sifton prepared the way for settlement by altering the land grant system through which speculators and coloni-zation companies had tied up much of the best land, by simplifying the process of securing homesteads, and by streamlining an organi-zation to administer his policy. The immigration promotion cam-paign that previous governments had initiated was given impetus in Europe and the United States and the government gave bonuses to steamship companies and agents who secured immigrants" (22).

22 See McClung's editorial in the *Western Home Monthly* (October 1921: 3) and "Nellie McClung on Women and Reconstruction" in *Maclean's* (July 1919: 92, 94). She articulates a slightly different point of view in the article "We Must Share," published late in her life in *More Leaves from Lantern Lane* (1937, 111–14): "No coun-try can hold back the urge of nations to expand. It will be a more carefully selected immigration, but we will have to open our doors" (112).

23 In *The Stream Runs Fast*, for instance, McClung describes the effects on Ukrainians of "the education given by ... missionaries": "The boys and girls learned about fresh air, and tooth brushes, board floors and more windows and improvements came naturally" (1945, 162).

24 Palmer notes that, under Sifton, the "immigration promotion campaign that previous governments had initiated was given impetus

in Europe and the United States and the government gave bonuses to steamship companies and agents who secured immigrants" (22).

25 See, for instance, the account of Helmi's striking of Martha with a tray (24–5) or the response of the first bad magistrate to Helmi's arrest (68). Finns are represented throughout the novel as "clean and neat, but high tempered" (25).

26 The designation "Galician" was used, with the term "Ruthenian," to refer, as Palmer notes, to Ukrainian peoples who "came from the province of Austria-Hungary known as Galicia" (28). The term "Galician," he also points out, "acquired more general connotations and was often used by the press and the public as a general category to refer to all immigrants from central and eastern Europe" (28). It was frequently used with a racist inflection: Woodsworth suggests in *Strangers within Our Gates* (1909), "In so low an estimation are they held that the word Galician is almost a term of reproach" (110).

McClung indicates that she had "thought first of taking a Ukrainian girl as [her] heroine" for *Painted Fires*, but had been "greatly attracted to Finland because of its advanced attitude to women" (*The Stream Runs Fast*, 237).

27 See *The Stream Runs Fast* (237–8) for McClung's sense of Finns as a people with "a passion for cleanliness."

28 See also Fiamengo, 76.

29 See, for instance, Bell, *Fighting the Traffic in Young Girls*.

30 Stead's series was entitled "The Maiden Tribute of Modern Babylon" and appeared in the *Pall Mall Gazette* over several days in July 1885.

31 See Devereux 2000.

32 See Pivar (1973), who draws attention to a WCTU article, "Another Maiden Tribute," about "a white slave trade in the Wisconsin and Michigan lumber camps" (136).

PART FOUR

1 Here, as below, Owram is citing William Clint, *The Aborigines of Canada under the British Crown* (1878), 178 and, below, 27.

2 The title of the first volume of McClung's autobiography, *Clearing in the West*, indicates both the space cleared by the Mooneys and the symbolic dawn of a new day, a familiar figure for imperial expansion. The first volume ends, "It was clearing in the West!

Tomorrow would be fine!" (378). There is a suggestion that the early Anglo-Saxon settlers in the West made this "new" day possible.

3 This pamphlet has no date but must precede the United Church Board of Home Missions pamphlet published in 1937, since it is published under the auspices of the Methodist Woman's Missionary Society and the Methodist Church was not amalgamated into the United Church until 1932. (The first union took place in 1907, with arguments for wider reunion in 1913.)

4 McClung's text for "Organized Helpfulness" appears in Woodsworth's autobiographical work, *Thirty Years in the Canadian North-West* (1917), 248–59.

5 On the concept of "darkness," see Patrick Brantlinger, 1988, *Rule of Darkness: British Literature and Imperialism, 1830–1914.*

6 Woodsworth's series on the sterilization of the "unfit" appeared in the *Manitoba Free Press* on 11 October; 1, 8, and 15 November, 1916.

7 In *Strangers within Our Gates* (1909), Woodsworth ranks immigrants by desirability according to their relative "Nordicity": Anglo-Saxons (British and American) head the list, followed in descending order by Scandinavians, western Europeans, eastern Europeans, "Levantine races," "Orientals," and, finally, "the Negro and the Indian." See his table of contents, 5–6.

8 McClung reiterates this infantilizing perception in an account of a 1907 trip with a Dominion Commission "to arrange Treaty No. 10 with the Saskatchewan Indians" in 1907 (214). The article, published in the propagandist magazine *Canada West* in 1911, begins with a representation of Métis Isidore Bouvier, "lazy, improvident, of a childlike simplicity – a lamentable heathen with a thirst" (213) – and thus, according to McClung, an easy dupe for "canny" white men who follow the commission to buy the scrip from the Métis. McClung's account is ambivalent: she sees the commission making an erstwhile attempt to provide the Métis with land, against "childlike" indifference and white crooks; moreover, while the objective of the treaty negotiation is the acquisition of land for white settlers, it is configured here as a work of restoring the "birthright" of the Métis people (218). See "Peddling Scrip to Lo," *Canada West* 10 (1907): 213–18.

9 McClung published a book of First World War writings with the title *The Next of Kin* (1917).

10 McClung, for instance, aligns German and English-Canadian women on several occasions, suggesting that these women are all "mothers," all sharing the same desire to protect their children and the world for their children and that men are the problem.

11 See for instance John S. Milloy, 1999, *A National Crime: The Canadian Government and the Residential School System, 1879–1986.*

12 McClung's brief support of racially limited votes for women in the 1917 Wartime Elections Act is not characteristic of her sense, articulated before 1917 in *In Times Like These* and after, that white women, "foreign" women and, as in "Red and White," First Nations women, should be enfranchised simultaneously.

EPILOGUE

1 See also McClung's editorial on "Naturalization" in the *Western Home Monthly*, October 1921, 3.

Bibliography

Most of McClung's papers are held by the British Columbia Archives in Victoria, B.C. (PABC). The 7.27 metres of records include correspondence, newspaper clippings, handwritten and typescript copies of published and unpublished works, notes for speeches, and scrapbooks. A finding aid is available online. Archival materials included in this bibliography are identified by box and file number.

"Alberta Board Had Assembly Line Sterilizations." 1995. *Canadian Press Newswire,* 23 June.

Althusser, Louis. 1977. "Ideology and Ideological State Apparatuses (Notes towards an Investigation)." In *Lenin and Philosophy and Other Essays,* 127–86. Translated by Ben Brewster. London: New Left Books.

Amos, Valerie, and Pratibha Parmar. 1984. "Imperial Feminism." *Feminist Review* 17: 3–19.

Anderson, Benedict. 1996. *Imagined Communities: Reflections on the Origin and Spread of Nationalism.* Rev. ed. London and New York: Verso.

Anderson, Kay J. 1995. *Vancouver's Chinatown: Racial Discourse in Canada, 1875–1980.* Kingston and Montreal: McGill-Queen's University Press.

Ardis, Anne L. 1990. *New Women, New Novels: Feminism and Early Modernism.* New Brunswick, N.J., and London: Rutgers University Press.

Bacchi, Carol Lee. 1983. *Liberation Deferred? The Ideas of the English-Canadian Suffragists, 1877–1918*. Toronto, Buffalo and London: University of Toronto Press.

– 1980. "Evolution, Eugenics and Women: The Impact of Scientific Theories on Attitudes towards Women, 1870–1920." In *Women, Class and History: Feminist Perspectives on Australia, 1788–1978*, edited by Elizabeth Windschuttle, 132–56. Melbourne: Fontana/Collins.

Backhouse, Constance. 1999. *Colour-Coded: A Legal History of Racism in Canada, 1900–1950*. Toronto: University of Toronto Press.

– 1991. *Petticoats and Prejudice: Women and Law in Nineteenth-Century Canada*. Toronto: Women's Press; New York: Dodd, Mead.

Baker, La Reine Helen. 1912. *Race Improvement and Eugenics: A Little Book on a Great Subject*. New York: Dodd, Mead and Co.

Barnes, David S. 1995. *The Making of a Social Disease: Tuberculosis in Nineteenth Century France*. Berkeley, Los Angeles and London: University of California Press.

Beall, Arthur W. 1933. *Manual on Eugenics for Parents and Teachers*. Whitby, Ont.: Penhale.

Bell, Ernest A., ed. *Fighting the Traffic in Young Girls, or War on the White Slave Trade*. 1910. Reprint, 1980, Toronto: Coles.

Benham, Mary Lile. 1984. *Nellie McClung*. Don Mills, Ont.: Fitzhenry and Whiteside.

Berger, Carl. 1970. *The Sense of Power: Studies in the Ideas of Canadian Imperialism, 1867–1914*. Toronto: University of Toronto Press.

– 1966. "The True North Strong and Free." In *Nationalism in Canada*, edited by Peter Russell, 3–26. Toronto: McGraw-Hill.

Bland, Lucy. 1995. *Banishing the Beast: Sexuality and the Early Feminists*. New York: New Press.

– 1987. "The Married Woman, the 'New Woman' and the Feminist: Sexual Politics of the 1890s." In *Equal or Different: Women's Politics, 1800–1914*, edited by Jane Rendall, 141–64. Oxford: Blackwell.

Brantlinger, Patrick. 1988. *Rule of Darkness: British Literature and Imperialism, 1830–1914*. Ithaca and London: Cornell University Press.

Burdett, Carolyn. 1998. "The Hidden Romance of Sexual Science: Eugenics, the Nation and the Making of Modern Feminism." In *Sexology in Culture: Labelling Bodies and Desires*, edited by Lucy Bland and Laura Doan, 44–59. Chicago: University of Chicago Press.

Burke, Richard M. 1938. *A Historical Chronology of Tuberculosis*. Springfield, Ill., and Baltimore, Md.: Charles C. Thomas.

Burton, Antoinette. 1994. *Burdens of History: British Feminists, Indian Women, and Imperial Culture, 1865–1915*. Chapel Hill and London: University of North Carolina Press.

– 1992. "The White Woman's Burden: British Feminists and 'The Indian Woman,'" 1865–1914. In *Western Women and Imperialism: Complicity and Resistance*, edited by Nupur Chaudhuri and Margaret Strobel, 137–57. Bloomington and Indiana: Indiana University Press.

Byfield, Ted. 1999. "Dubious Heroes: Let's Hope the 21st Century Unmasks the Flawed Perceptions of the 20th." *Alberta Report* 26, no. 25: 44.

Cameron, Agnes Dean. 1907. "The Empire of the Larger Hope." *Canada West* (July): 348–56.

Carter, Sarah. 1997. *Capturing Women: The Manipulation of Cultural Imagery in Canada's Prairie West*. Montreal and Kingston: McGill-Queen's University Press.

Chapman, Terry. 1977. "Early Eugenics Movement in Western Canada." *Alberta History* 25, no. 4: 9–17.

Chaudhuri, Nupur, and Margaret Strobel, eds. 1992. *Western Women and Imperialism: Complicity and Resistance*. Bloomington and Indianapolis: Indiana University Press.

Cleverdon, Catherine L. 1974. *The Woman Suffrage Movement in Canada*. 1950. Introduction by Ramsay Cook. Toronto: University of Toronto Press.

Connor, Ralph. 1909. *The Foreigner*. Toronto: Westminster.

Davin, Anna. 1978. "Imperialism and Motherhood." *History Workshop Journal* 5: 9–65.

Davis, Marilyn I. 1996. Introduction to *Stories Subversive: Through the Fields with Gloves Off. Short Fiction by Nellie L. McClung*, edited by Marilyn I. Davis, 1–34. Ottawa: University of Ottawa Press.

– 1991. "Fiction of a Feminist: Nellie McClung's Work for Children." *Canadian Children's Literature* 62: 37–59.

Davis, Marilyn I., and Mary Hallett. 1994. *Firing the Heather: The Life and Times of Nellie McClung*. Saskatoon: Fifth House.

Dean, Misao. 1998. *Practising Femininity: Domestic Realism and the Performance of Gender in Early Canadian Fiction*. Toronto: University of Toronto Press.

Devereux, Cecily. 2003. "'Not One of Those Dreadful New Women': Anne Shirley and the Culture of Imperial Motherhood." In *Windows and Words: A Look at Canadian Children's Literature in English*, edited by Aïda Hudson and Susan-Ann Cooper. Ottawa: University of Ottawa Press.

– 2001. "Writing with a 'Definite Purpose': L.M. Montgomery, Nellie L. McClung and the Politics of Imperial Motherhood in Fiction for Children." *Canadian Children's Literature* 99, no. 3: 6–22.

– 2000. "'The Maiden Tribute' and the Rise of the White Slave in the Nineteenth Century: The Making of an Imperial Construct." *Victorian Review* 26, no. 2: 1–23.

– 1999. "New Woman, New World: Maternal Feminism and the New Imperialism in the White Settler Colonies." In *Women's Studies International Forum* 22, no. 2: 175–84.

Dilke, Charles. 1869. *Greater Britain: A Record of Travel in English-Speaking Countries during 1866 and 1867.* New York: Harper.

Dowbiggin, Ian. 1998. Column. *Globe and Mail,* 3 July: A23.

Dubos, Rene, and Jean. 1952. *The White Plague: Tuberculosis, Man and Society.* Boston: Little, Brown.

Duncan, Sara Jeannette. 1908. *Cousin Cinderella.* Reprint, 1994, Ottawa: Tecumseh.

– 1906. *Set in Authority.* Reprint, 1996, edited by Germaine Warkentin. Peterborough, Ont.: Broadview.

– 1901. *On the Other Side of the Latch.* London: Methuen.

Ellis, Havelock. 1931. *More Essays of Love and Virtue.* New York: Doubleday Doran.

– 1914. *The Task of Social Hygiene.* Boston and New York: Houghton Mifflin.

– 1904. *Study of British Genius.* New edition, 1926. Boston and New York: Houghton Mifflin.

"Eugenical Sterilization in Canada." 1928. *Eugenical News* 13, no. 4 (April): 47–8.

Fiamengo, Janice. 1999–2000. "A Legacy of Contradiction: Responses to Nellie McClung." *Journal of Canadian Studies* 34, no. 4: 70–87.

Forget, Henriette. 1900. "The Indian Women of the Western Provinces." In *Women of Canada: Their Life and Work,* 435–7. National Council of Women of Canada.

Galton, Francis. 1869. *Hereditary Genius: An Inquiry into Its Laws and Consequences.* London: Macmillan.

Ghosh, Sabitri. 1999. "Monumental Questions: The Human Rights Legacy of the Famous Five." *Catholic New Times* 23, no. 15:10–11.

Gilman, Charlotte Perkins. 1911. *The Man-Made World, or Our Androcentric Culture.* New York: Charlton. Reprint, 1971, New York and London: Johnson.

– 1898. *Women and Economics*. Reprint, New York: Harper and Row.

Glazier, Lynn. 1992. "Playing God: Medical Ethics and History's Forgotten Issues." Transcript, CBC *Sunday Morning*.

Gorham, Deborah. 1976. "The Canadian Suffragists." In *Women in the Canadian Mosaic*, edited by Gwen Matheson, 23–56. Toronto: Peter Martin.

Haliburton, R.G. 1869. "The Men of the North and Their Place in History." Montreal: John Lovell.

Hammerton, James. 1979. *Emigrant Gentlewomen: Genteel Poverty and Female Emigration, 1830–1914*. London: Croom Helm.

– 1977. "Feminism and Female Emigration." In *A Widening Sphere*, edited by Martha Vicinus, 52–71. Bloomington: Indiana University Press.

Hancock, Carol. 1986. *No Small Legacy*. Winfield, B.C.: Wood Lake.

Hathaway, E.J. 1919. "How Canadian Novelists Are Using Canadian Opportunities." *Canadian Bookman* (July): 18–22.

Hawkes, Arthur. 1919. *The Birthright: A Search for the Canadian Canadian and the Larger Loyalty*. Toronto: Dent.

Hobsbawm, E.J. 1990. *Nations and Nationalism Since 1780: Programme, Myth, Reality*. 2nd ed. Cambridge: Cambridge University Press.

Huber, John Bessner. 1906. *Consumption: Its Relation to Man and His Civilization*. Philadelphia and London: Lippincott.

Inglis, Amirah. 1975. *The White Women's Protection Ordinance: Sexual Anxiety and Politics in Papua*. New York: St Martin's.

Jackel, Susan. 1987. *Canadian Prairie Women's History: A Bibliographic Survey*. Ottawa: CRIAW/ICREF.

– 1982. *A Flannel Shirt and Liberty: British Emigrant Gentlewomen in the Canadian West, 1880–1914*. Vancouver: University of British Columbia Press.

Jayawardena, Kumari. 1995. *The White Woman's Other Burden: Western Women and South Asia during British Colonial Rule*. New York and London: Routledge.

Johnson, E. Pauline. 1913. "Mother o' the Men." In *The Moccasin Maker*. Reprint, 1998, introduced by A. LaVonne Brown Ruoff, 180–94. Norman, Okla.: University of Oklahoma Press.

Kevles, Daniel J. 1985. *In the Name of Eugenics: Genetics and the Uses of Human Heredity*. New York: Knopf.

Lakritz, Naomi. 1999. Column. *Calgary Herald*, 19 October: A27.

Lambert, Norman P. 1916. "A Joan of the West." *Canadian Magazine*: 265–8.

Lawson, Olive, ed. 1990. *The First Voice of Australian Feminism: Excerpts from Louisa Lawson's* The Dawn, *1888–1895.* Melbourne: Simon and Schuster.

Leacock, Stephen. 1915. "The Woman Question." *Maclean's* (October): 7–9.

Lighthall, W.D. 1889. *Songs of the Great Dominion.* Reprint, 1971, Toronto: Coles.

Lochhead, W.L. 1919. "Genetics – The Science of Breeding." *Canadian Bookman* (July): 65–6.

Logan, J.D., and Donald French. 1924. *Highways of Canadian Literature: A Synoptic Introduction to the Literary History of Canada (English) from 1760 to 1924.* Toronto: McClelland and Stewart.

Machar, Agnes Maule. 1892. *Marjorie's Canadian Winter: A Story of the Northern Lights.* Boston: D. Lothrop.

– 1870. *Katie Johnstone's Cross.* Toronto: J. Campbell.

McClintock, Anne. 1995. *Imperial Leather: Race, Gender, and Sexuality in the Colonial Contest.* New York: Routledge.

McClung, Nellie L. N.d. "Woman's Place in the Bandwagon." PABC MS-0010, box 24, file 3: 227–34.

– N.d. Speech: "Radio." PABC MS-0010, box 25, file 8.

– N.d. "The Writer's Creed." PABC MS-0010, box 24, file 5: 158–64.

– 1996. *Stories Subversive: Through the Fields with Gloves Off. Short Fiction by Nellie L. McClung.* Edited by Marilyn I. Davis. Ottawa: University of Ottawa Press.

– 1945. *The Stream Runs Fast: My Own Story.* Toronto: Thomas Allen.

– 1937a. "Before They Call." Board of Home Missions: The United Church of Canada.

– 1937b. "We Must Share." In *More Leaves from Lantern Lane.* Toronto: Thomas Allen, 111–14.

– 1936. *Leaves from Lantern Lane.* Toronto: Thomas Allen.

– 1935. *Clearing in the West: My Own Story.* Toronto: Thomas Allen.

– 1930. *Be Good to Yourself and Other Stories.* Toronto: Thomas Allen.

– 1928. "Can a Woman Raise a Family and Have a Career?" *Maclean's* (15 February).

– [1927]. "An Insistent Call." United Church Archives, Victoria College, Toronto.

– 1926. *All We Like Sheep and Other Stories.* Toronto: Thomas Allen.

– 1925. *Painted Fires.* Toronto: Thomas Allen.

– 1924. Speech in Alberta Legislature, 31 January. PABC MS-0010, box 25, file 7.

- 1923. *When Christmas Crossed "The Peace."* Toronto: Thomas Allen.
- 1921–22. "Red and White." *Western Home Monthly* (November 1921): 4–5; (December 1921): 2; (January 1922): 4; (February 1922): 4, 8–9.
- 1921a. "Naturalization." *Western Home Monthly* (October): 3.
- 1921b. "Eighth Day, Tuesday, September 13. First Session. Topic: Women's Work." *Proceedings of the Fifth Ecumenical Methodist Conference, September 6–16, 1921.* Toronto: Methodist Book and Publishing House.
- 1921c. *Purple Springs.* Toronto: Thomas Allen.
- 1919a. "Listen – Ladies!" *Everywoman's World* (June): 18, 63.
- 1919b. "Nellie McClung on Women and Reconstruction." *Maclean's* (July): 92–4.
- 1918. *Three Times and Out.* Told by Private Mervin C. Simmons; written by Nellie L. McClung. Toronto: Thomas Allen.
- 1917. *The Next of Kin.* Toronto: Thomas Allen.
- 1916a. "What Will They Do with It?" *Maclean's* (July): 36–8.
- 1916b. "Speaking of Women." *Maclean's* (May): 25–6, 96–7.
- 1915. *In Times Like These.* Toronto: McLeod and Allen.
- 1912a. *The Black Creek Stopping-House and Other Stories.* Toronto: Briggs.
- 1912b. "Organized Helpfulness: All People's Mission, 1911–12." Winnipeg: The Winnipeg Church Extension and City Mission Association of the Methodist Church.
- 1911. "Peddling Scrip to Lo." *Canada West* 10: 213–18.
- 1910. *The Second Chance.* Toronto: William Briggs.
- 1908. *Sowing Seeds in Danny.* Toronto: Briggs.
- 1907. "Babette." *Canada West* 2 (November): 49–52.

McCuaig, Katherine. 1999. *The Weariness, the Fever, and the Fret: The Campaign against Tuberculosis in Canada, 1900–1950.* Montreal and Kingston: McGill-Queen's University Press.

McLaren, Angus. 1990. *Our Own Master Race: Eugenics in Canada, 1885–1945.* Toronto: McClelland and Stewart.

MacMurchy Willison, Marjorie. 1916. *The Woman, Bless Her: Not As Amiable a Book As It Sounds.* Toronto: Gundy.

Mangum, Teresa. 1998. *Married, Middlebrow, and Militant: Sarah Grand and the New Woman Novel.* Ann Arbor: University of Michigan Press.

Matheson, Gwen, ed. 1976. *Women in the Canadian Mosaic.* Toronto: Peter Martin.

Matheson, Gwen, and V.E. Lang. 1976. "Nellie McClung: 'Not a Nice Woman.'" In *Women in the Canadian Mosaic,* edited by Gwen Matheson, 1–22. Toronto: Peter Martin.

Midgley, Clare, ed. 1998. *Gender and Imperialism*. Manchester University Press.

Miller, J.O., ed. 1917. *The New Era in Canada*. London, Paris, Toronto: Dent.

Milloy, John S. 1999. *A National Crime: The Canadian Government and the Residential School System, 1879–1986*. Winnipeg: University of Manitoba Press.

Mohanty, Chandra Talpade. 1984. "Under Western Eyes: Feminist Scholarship and Colonial Discourses." *Boundary* 2 12, no. 3 and 13, no. 1: 333–58.

Monkman, Leslie. 1981. *A Native Heritage: Images of the Indian in English-Canadian Literature*. Toronto: University of Toronto Press.

Montgomery, L.M. 1974. "Penelope Struts Her Theories." In *The Road to Yesterday*, 81–109. Toronto: McGraw Hill Ryerson.

– 1920. "Tannis of the Flats." In *Further Chronicles of Avonlea*. Reprint, 1987, Toronto: McClelland-Bantam.

– 1915. *Anne of the Island*. Reprint, 1976, New York: Bantam.

– 1908. *Anne of Green Gables*. Reprint, n.d., Toronto: McClelland-Bantam.

– 1891. "A Western Eden." *Prince Albert Times*, 17 June: 4.

Moore, George. 1894. *Esther Waters*. Reprint, 1983, London: Dent.

Murphy, Emily. 1932. "Sterilization of the Insane." *Vancouver Sun*, 3 September: 3.

– 1934. "Should the Unfit Wed?" *Vancouver Sun*, 10 September: 4.

– 1932. "Overpopulation and Birth Control." *Vancouver Sun*, 1 October: 2.

– 1925. Letter from Emily Murphy to George Hoadley, 20 April 1925. PABC MS-0010, box 11, file 8.

– 1922. *The Black Candle*. Toronto: Thomas Allen.

Murray, Georgina. 1997. "Agonize, Don't Organize: A Critique of Post-feminism." *Current Sociology* 45, no. 2, 37–48.

"Nellie McClung." 1993. *Heritage Minutes*. CRB Foundation, Montreal.

Newsholme, Arthur. 1910. *The Prevention of Tuberculosis*. London: Methuen.

"No End to Doing Good." 1995. *Western Report* 10, no. 24: 38–41.

"Nobody Has the Right to Play God." 1995. *Maclean's* 108, no. 26: 17.

"100 Most Important Canadians: Nellie McClung." 1999. *Maclean's* (1 July): 42–3.

"Our Heroes." 1999. Dominion Institute/Council for Canadian Unity.

Owram, Doug. 1980. *Promise of Eden: The Canadian Expansionist Movement and the Idea of the West, 1856–1900*. Toronto: University of Toronto Press.

Palmer, Howard. 1982. *Patterns of Prejudice: A History of Nativism in Alberta*. Toronto: McClelland and Stewart.

"Past Crusades Have Come Back to Haunt Us in the Courts: Leilani Muir Case." 1996. *Financial Post* 90, no. 4: 20.

Pierson, Ruth Roach, and Nupur Chaudhuri, eds. 1999. *Nation, Empire, Colony: Historicizing Gender and Race*. Bloomington and Indianapolis: Indiana University Press.

Pivar, David J. 1973. *Purity Crusade: Sexual Morality and Social Control, 1868–1900*. Westport, Conn.: Greenwood.

Pringle, Heather. 1997. "Alberta Barren." *Saturday Night* 112, no. 5: 30–37.

Revised Statutes of Alberta. 1942. Alberta Government Printer.

Roberts, Barbara. 1979. "'A Work of Empire': Canadian Reformers and British Female Immigration." In *A Not Unreasonable Claim: Women and Reform in Canada, 1880–1920s*, edited by Linda Kealey, 185–201. Toronto: Canadian Women's and Educational Press.

Roberts, Wayne. 1979. "'Rocking the Cradle for the World': The New Woman and Maternal Feminism, Toronto, 1877–1914." In *A Not Unreasonable Claim: Women and Reform in Canada, 1880–1920s*, edited by Linda Kealey, 15–45. Toronto: Canadian Women's and Educational Press.

Robins, Elizabeth. 1913. *Where Are You Going To...?* London: Heinemann.

Rothman, Sheila M. 1994. *Living in the Shadow of Death: Tuberculosis and the Social Experience of Illness in American History*. Baltimore and London: Johns Hopkins University Press.

Saleeby, Caleb W. 1924. *Sunlight and Health*. New York and London: Putnam's.

– 1921. *The Eugenic Prospect: National and Racial*. London: Fisher Unwin.

– 1911. *Woman and Womanhood: A Search for Principles*. New York and London: Mitchell Kennerley.

– 1911. *The Methods of Race-Regeneration*. London, New York: Cassell.

– 1909. *Parenthood and Race Culture: An Outline of Eugenics*. London, New York: Cassell.

Savage, Candace. 1985. *Our Nell: A Scrapbook Biography of Nellie L. McClung*. Halifax, N.S.: Goodread.

Scharlieb, Mary. 1912. *Womanhood and Race-Regeneration*. New York: Moffat, Yard.

"Scharlieb, Mary." 1937. *Dictionary of National Biography, Twentieth Century, 1922–1930.* Edited by J.R.H. Weaver. London: Oxford University Press, Humphrey Milford.

Schreiner, Olive. 1911. *Woman and Labour.* London: Unwin.

Scrapbook Hansard. 1922–24. Alberta Legislature, 2 February 1922–12 April 1924.

Semmel, Bernard. 1960. *Imperialism and Social Reform: English Social-Imperial Thought, 1895–1914.* Cambridge, Mass.: Harvard University Press.

Seton, Ernest Thompson. 1908. "The White Man's Last Opportunity." *Canada West* (April): 525–32.

Shepherd, Charles. 1923. *The Ways of Ah Sin: A Composite Narrative of Things As They Are.* New York and Chicago: Revell.

Spivak, Gayatri Chakravorty. 1985. "Three Women's Texts and a Critique of Imperialism." In *Feminisms.* Rev. ed., 1997, by Robyn R. Warhol and Diane Price Herndl, 896–912. New Brunswick, N.J.: Rutgers University Press.

Stead, W.T. 1894. "The Novel of the Modern Woman." *Review of Reviews* 10: 64–74.

– 1885. "The Maiden Tribute of Modern Babylon." *Pall Mall Gazette* (July): 4, 6, 7, 8, 10.

"Sterilization Law Had Wide Support (in 1928)." 1995. *Canadian Press Newswire,* 27 June.

The Sterilization of Leilani Muir. 1996. Videocassette. Montreal: NFB.

Stoler, Ann Laura. 1997. "Making Empire Respectable: The Politics of Race and Sexual Morality in Twentieth-Century Colonial Cultures." In *Dangerous Liaisons: Gender, Nation, and Postcolonial Perspectives,* edited byAnne McClintock, Aamir Mufti, and Ella Shohat, 344–73. Minneapolis and London: University of Minnesota Press.

Strachey, John. 1959–60. *The End of Empire.* New York: Praeger.

Strong-Boag, Veronica. 1991. "'Ever a Crusader': Nellie McClung, First-Wave Feminist." In *Rethinking Canada: The Promise of Women's History,* edited by Veronica Strong-Boag and Anita Clair, 308–21. Fellman. Toronto: Copp Clark Pitman.

– 1972. Introduction to *In Times Like These,* by Nellie McClung. Toronto: University of Toronto Press.

Thomas, Clara. 1978. "Women Writers and the New Land." In *The New Land: Studies in a Literary Theme,* edited by Richard Chadbourne and Hallbard Dahlie, 45–60. Waterloo: Wilfrid Laurier University Press.

Tri-Country Anti-Tuberculosis League of Antigonish, Guysborough, and Pictou. 1911. *Consumption: Its Cause, Prevention, and Cure.* London: Eyre and Spottiswoode.

Turner, George Kibbe. 1909–10. "The Daughters of the Poor." *McClure's* 34 (November 1909-April 1910): 45–61.

Valverde, Mariana. 1992. "'When the Mother of the Race Is Free': Race, Reproduction, and Sexuality in First-Wave Feminism." In *Gender Conflicts: New Essays in Women's History*, edited by Franca Iacovetta and Mariana Valverde, 3–26. Toronto: University of Toronto Press.

– 1991. *The Age of Light, Soap, and Water: Moral Reform in English Canada, 1885–1925.* Toronto: McClelland and Stewart.

Verkuysse, Patricia. 1975. "Small Legacy of Truth: The Novels of Nellie McClung." Master's thesis, University of New Brunswick.

"A Victim of Eugenics Fights Back." 1998. *Western Report* 8, no. 22: 38.

Ware, Vron. 1992. *Beyond the Pale: White Women, Racism and History.* London and New York: Verso.

Warne, Randi R. 1995. "Nellie McClung's Social Gospel." In *Changing Roles of Women within the Christian Church in Canada*, edited by Elizabeth Gillian Muir and Marilyn Färdig Whiteley, 338–54. Toronto: University of Toronto Press.

– 1993. *Literature As Pulpit: The Christian Social Activism of Nellie L. McClung.* Waterloo, Ont.: Wilfrid Laurier University Press.

– 1992. Introduction to *Purple Springs*, by Nellie L. McClung. Toronto: University of Toronto Press.

"What Women Say of the Canadian North-West." 1886. Montreal: N.p.

Whetham, William C.D., and Catherine D. Whetham. 1909. *The Family and the Nation: A Study in Natural Inheritance and Social Responsibility.* London: Longman's, Green.

Woodward, Joe. "But She Was a Feminist Racist." 1998. *British Columbia Report* 9, no. 38: 30.

Woodsworth, James S. 1909. *Strangers within Our Gates, or Coming Canadians.* Reprint, 1972, edited and introduced by Marilyn Barber. Toronto: University of Toronto Press.

Woodsworth, James. 1917. *Thirty Years in the Canadian North-West.* Toronto: McClelland, Goodchild and Stewart.

Wright, Helen K. 1980. *Nellie McClung and Women's Rights.* Agincourt, Ont.: Book Society of Canada.

Index